THE

RIDGEWAY

NATIONAL TRAIL COMPANION

supported by

2nd edition published February 2002

© National Trails Office

ISBN 0-9535207-3-0

Edited by Jos Joslin & Rebecca Wilson

Photographs by Jos Joslin

Published by

National Trails Office

Cultural Services

Holton

Oxford OX33 1QQ

tel 01865 810224

fax 01865 810207

email mail@rway-tpath.demon.co.uk

website www.nationaltrails.gov.uk

Produced by Leap Frog Communications Ltd

Designed by Linda Francis

Cover photo:

Looking south from Hackpen Hill, Wiltshire

Contents

I Introduction   5

II History   8

III Wildlife   9

IV Using The Ridgeway   11

V Finding Your Way   13

VI Publications   15

VII Useful Contacts   16

VIII Getting There   20

IX Respect the Countryside   21

X Emergency Contacts   22

XI Accommodation, Facilities & Services   24

Section 1 – Overton Hill to Uffington Castle   29

Section 2 – Uffington Castle to Streatley   49

Section 3 – Streatley to Chinnor   65

Section 4 – Chinnor to Ivinghoe Beacon   81

Index of Places   95

Distances between places   96

Folly Clump in the distance, south of Childrey

Looking from Ladies Walk to Jacob's tent, Swyncombe

Introduction

One hundred and thirty six kilometres (85 miles) long, much of it following the ancient chalk ridge route used by prehistoric man and surrounded by numerous historic monuments, The Ridgeway offers the chance to get away from the bustle of life in this busy part of England. Perfect, but not too strenuous, for long distance use, this Trail is also ideal for day trips or less. The whole of The Ridgeway can be enjoyed by walkers with horseriders and cyclists able to use all of the western half as far as the River Thames at Streatley and short sections further east.

The Ridgeway

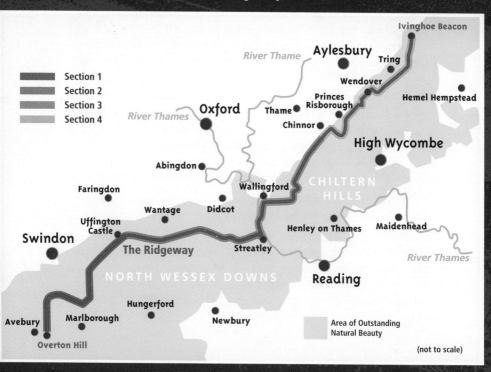

Section 1
Section 2
Section 3
Section 4

Ivinghoe Beacon
River Thame
Aylesbury
Tring
Wendover
Princes Risborough
Hemel Hempstead
River Thames
Oxford
Thame
Chinnor
High Wycombe
Abingdon
CHILTERN HILLS
Faringdon
Wallingford
Wantage
Didcot
Uffington Castle
Henley on Thames
Maidenhead
Swindon
The Ridgeway
Streatley
River Thames
NORTH WESSEX DOWNS
Reading
Hungerford
Avebury
Marlborough
Newbury
Area of Outstanding Natural Beauty
Overton Hill
(not to scale)

I INTRODUCTION

Welcome to the Ridgeway Companion. It provides up-to-date practical information about accommodation, refreshments and many other facilities along this National Trail. The Companion is designed to help with planning anything from a week's holiday to a short walk or ride.

The Companion is not a route guide: for detailed information about the Trail itself, The Ridgeway National Trail Guide by Neil Curtis (Aurum Press, 2001) is available from most book shops or from Amazon via the internet. Alternatively it can be mail ordered from the National Trails Office (see page 16 for details). The Companion complements the Trail Guide and, armed with a copy of each, it is hoped that anyone using The Ridgeway needn't require anything more. Enjoy your trip.

One of only 15 National Trails in England and Wales, The Ridgeway starts in the famous World Heritage Site of Avebury in Wiltshire and travels for 136 km (85 miles) steadily north east along the surprisingly remote scarp ridge of the downs, across the River Thames, and through the Chiltern Hills to finish in the Iron Age fort on top of Ivinghoe Beacon in Buckinghamshire.

The western half of The Ridgeway, as far as Streatley on Thames, can be enjoyed by walkers, horseriders and cyclists, whereas only walkers can use the full extent of the eastern half. Despite its relative remoteness, public transport to The Ridgeway is pretty good, especially to the eastern half, where there are several railway stations close to the Trail and an excellent bus network. With a little planning many places along the western half can also be reached by bus or train or a combination of the two.

The Ridgeway passes through two distinctive landscapes; the open downland of the west and the more gentle and wooded countryside of the Chiltern Hills in the east.

In the west The Ridgeway travels as a broad ancient track along the open and fairly isolated top of the chalk downland ridge, often several kilometres from the nearest village. Here, to the south is rolling downland and to the north, at the bottom of the steep scarp slope, the wide expanse of the Thames Valley. The far-reaching views are dominated by the sky, the clouds and small clumps of beech woodland and all you may have for company is a solitary skylark singing overhead or a hare chasing across an adjacent field.

In the past these downs were sheep grazed, but since the introduction of fertilisers earlier this century many areas have been ploughed and planted with crops. However sheep grazing does continue in places and, in others, a characteristic sight is immaculately managed grass tracks, the gallops used for training racehorses. The excellent turf of the downs makes this prime horse country but you need to be up early to see the strings of racehorses exercising.

At Streatley The Ridgeway crosses the River Thames, and another of England's National Trails, the Thames Path, entering more intimate and less open countryside. It follows the bank of this famous river along a lovely 8 km (5 miles) rural stretch before heading eastwards into the Chiltern Hills. Mostly on narrower paths, the Trail passes through woodlands, many of them beech, over neatly cultivated fields and across chalk grassland nature reserves rich in wildflowers. In contrast to the western half, although its usually peaceful here, you're never far from pleasant small towns or attractive villages.

With the support of the Countryside Agency, The Ridgeway is managed to the highest standards necessary for one of the most important paths in the country by the local highway authorities with a small dedicated team of staff.

Wayland's Smithy, a New Stone Age long barrow 2 km (1.2 miles) southwest of Uffington Castle

II HISTORY

For thousands of years, at least 5,000 and maybe many more, people have walked or ridden The Ridgeway, be they drovers, traders, invaders or today's recreational visitors. As part of a prehistoric track once stretching about 400 km (250 miles) from the Dorset coast to the Wash on the Norfolk coast, The Ridgeway provided a route over the high ground for travellers which was less wooded and drier than routes through the springline villages below.

New Stone Age men, the first farmers in Britain, left the earliest remains. Their long barrows can be found at a few places both west and east of the River Thames. It was Bronze Age people from later times, around 2,000 BC, however, who dragged the huge sarsen stones from the surrounding hills and formed the dramatic Avebury Circle. There are many of their round burial barrows along the length of the National Trail.

Hill forts built during the Iron Age from about 500 BC until the Romans arrived in 43 AD are also found both sides of the Thames. These forts command the high ground and in several places they defended The Ridgeway against attack from the north.

In the Dark Ages The Ridgeway was a main route for the Saxons and Vikings who fought many battles during their advances into Wessex. In medieval times it was drovers driving livestock from Wales and the West Country to the Home Counties, not armies, who used The Ridgeway.

Until the Enclosure Acts of 1750 The Ridgeway was a broad band of tracks along the crest of the downs where travellers chose the driest or most convenient path. During Enclosures the exact course and width of The Ridgeway was defined by the building of earth banks and the planting of thorn hedges to prevent livestock straying into the newly cultivated fields.

In recent times use of The Ridgeway has changed greatly: farmers do still use much of it as an access route to their fields for tractors and other machinery but its main use is no longer utilitarian but recreational with walkers and riders out for exercise, pleasure and spiritual refreshment.

The grasslands which occur on the chalk of the downs and the Chiltern Hills are some of the most interesting habitats in England and some of the richest in terms of the number of plant species found. Chalk grassland has suffered from modern farming and much has disappeared under the plough. However those unimproved chalk grassland areas along The Ridgeway, especially the nature reserves east of the Thames, are well worth visiting where you'll find, amongst many other lovely plants, several types of orchid.

Another botanical treat in store for visitors during springtime is the carpet of bluebells in many of the woodlands in the Chiltern Hills, usually in the first couple of weeks of May.

For those keen on seeing birds, The Ridgeway should not disappoint you. A range of relatively common birds such as warblers and finches are found the length of The Ridgeway enjoying the food supply provided by the hedges lining the Trail. Skylarks, yellowhammers and corn buntings are particularly characteristic of the downland and although generally in decline in Britain are still numerous along The Ridgeway. The song of the corn bunting, likened to the sound of a jangle of keys, is the distinctive sound of the western half of The Ridgeway.

In colder months flocks of redwing and fieldfare, winter visitors from Scandinavia, are common and are usually seen feeding in the fields surrounding the Trail. However, most people will especially cherish the site of a red kite and you'll be unlucky if you don't see one in the Chiltern Hills. These magnificent birds of prey recognised by their forked tail were reintroduced to this area in the late 1980s and are now well established. In woodlands of this area too, woodpeckers and nuthatches may well be spotted.

Apart from the ubiquitous rabbit, hares and deer are the larger wild animals you may encounter. Hares are found in open countryside and are bigger than rabbits with longer ears and hind legs. They are solitary animals and most active at night, so late evening or early morning are the best times to see them. Two species of deer are found on The Ridgeway, roe and fallow with the former being the smaller and also living in smaller groups of just three or four animals. Both of these species are nocturnal and shy so, as for hares, being on The Ridgeway at dusk or dawn will give you the best chance of viewing them.

Southwest of Sparsholt

St Botolph's Swyncombe, an early Norman church dedicated to the patron saint of travellers

The Ridgeway provides excellent walking, cycling and horse riding opportunities although it is only walkers who can use the whole length of the Trail.

Cyclists and Horseriders

Riders, both cyclists and horseriders, can share The Ridgeway with walkers all the way from the start at Overton Hill near Avebury to Streatley on the River Thames, a distance of roughly 68 km (43 miles). Once across the river the only long section of the Trail which can be ridden is the 13 km (8 miles) stretch which follows the Icknield Way through the Chilterns from Britwell Hill near Watlington to Wainhill on the Oxfordshire/Buckinghamshire border. In other places The Ridgeway is a footpath and it is a trespass offence to ride on a footpath without the permission of the landowner.

However an alternative for riders is to join the Swan's Way long distance bridleway at Goring on Thames, just across the river from Streatley, and to follow this, mostly on The Ridgeway to Bledlow west of Princes Risborough (here the Swan's Way turns north). From Bledlow riders can pick up the Icknield Way Riders' Route which provides a good alternative to The Ridgeway for riders as far as Pitstone Hill, just a couple of kilometres from Ivinghoe Beacon. Unfortunately riders can't continue to Ivinghoe Beacon, the official end of the National Trail, since the route to it is on footpaths.

Vehicles

It's worth knowing, so that it doesn't come as a surprise to see a motorbike or four wheel drive, that vehicles can legally use most of the western half of The Ridgeway and a few sections east of the Thames. However recreational vehicles and motorcycles only comprise about 5% of the total usage of The Ridgeway with agricultural vehicles another 1%, so you're unlikely to meet too many vehicles.

Code of Respect

A Code of Respect has been operating on The Ridgeway for the last few years to encourage all users to act responsibly to conserve the Trail and to be aware and considerate of the rights of others. Details of the Code are shown on page 18 and you are asked to familiarise yourself with it before visiting The Ridgeway.

IV USING THE RIDGEWAY

Be prepared!

When venturing into the countryside it is wise to be prepared for the elements: even in summer, wind and rain can make a walk or ride cold and uncomfortable, so suitable warm and waterproof clothing should be worn or carried in a small rucksack. In the summer, especially on much of the western half of The Ridgeway which is exposed, it is also advisable to wear protection against the sun and to carry a water bottle since water points are relatively infrequent (see each section for information on these).

From April to the end of October most years The Ridgeway is usually dry with conditions on the whole good. There are, however, places where ruts have developed and care needs to be taken, so do wear strong, comfortable footwear. From November to March parts of The Ridgeway can become muddy making it difficult in places to walk or cycle - on the whole you'll find that the footpath sections are fine.

 ### Dog Matters

If you are planning to undertake a long distance walk along The Ridgeway with your dog, you are advised to ensure it is fit before you start; on occasions walkers have had to abandon a walk because their dogs can't keep up!

Please also make sure your dog is under close control at all times to prevent it from disturbing livestock or wildlife. You are asked to keep your dog on a lead when you're in the few fields you'll encounter with livestock, although if you find that cattle seriously harass you because of the dog, it may be wise to let it off the lead.

Signing

The Ridgeway follows a series of well-signed public rights of way along which people have legal right of access.

An acorn, the symbol of Britain's National Trails, is used to guide your journey by marking the route in a variety of ways. It is used in conjunction with coloured arrows or the words 'footpath', 'bridleway' or 'byway' to indicate who can use a particular right of way.

The word 'footpath' and/or a yellow arrow indicates a path for use by walkers only and where, without the landowner's permission, it is illegal to cycle, ride a horse or drive a vehicle.

The word 'bridleway' and/or a blue arrow indicates a path which can be used by walkers, horseriders and cyclists but where, without the landowner's permission, it is illegal to drive any vehicle.

The word 'byway' and/or a red arrow indicates a right of way which can be legally used by walkers, horseriders, cyclists and motorists.

The Ridgeway is signposted where it crosses roads and other rights of way using mostly recycled plastic materials. Elsewhere, waymark discs with acorns and coloured arrows are used on gates and waymark posts.

Guides

'The Ridgeway National Trail Guide by Neil Curtis', Aurum Press, updated 2001 and costing £12.99 is the official guide with written route description and colour 1:25 000 maps.

Harvey Maps publish 'Ridgeway', a detailed waterproof map at the scale of 1:40 000 of the entire National Trail which includes locations of facilities and services close to the Trail. It costs £8.95.

V FINDING YOUR WAY

Maps

It is usually a good idea to use maps when walking, particularly in unfamiliar areas. The National Trail Guide includes colour sections of all the appropriate 1:25 000 Ordnance Survey maps needed to follow The Ridgeway. Alternatively, for you to enjoy and interpret the wider landscape, you may wish to purchase your own Ordnance Survey maps.

The Landranger series (pink cover at 1:50 000 or 2 cm to 1 km) has all public rights of way, viewpoints, tourist information and selected places of interest marked on them. For the whole of The Ridgeway you will need:

173   Swindon and Devizes
174   Newbury and Wantage
175   Reading and Windsor
165   Aylesbury and Leighton Buzzard

The larger scale Explorer series (orange cover at 1:25 000 or 4 cm to 1 km) has more detail including fence lines which can be very helpful when following rights of way, recreational routes and greater tourist information. For the whole of The Ridgeway you will need:

157   Marlborough and Savernake Forest
170   Abingdon, Wantage and Vale of White Horse
171   Chiltern Hills West
181   Chiltern Hills North

A typical Coombe

Publications About The Ridgeway

Below is a selection of publications about The Ridgeway:

The Ridgeway National Trail Guide by Neil Curtis, Aurum Press, updated 2001 - the official guide with written route description and colour 1:25 000 maps. Available from the National Trails Office.

Ridgeway, Harvey Maps, 1999 - 1:40 000 scale waterproof map of the entire route of The Ridgeway including information on a range of facilities along the Trail. Available from the National Trails Office.

Exploring the Ridgeway by Alan Charles, Countryside Books, updated 2000 - based on 14 circular walks covering the whole length of The Ridgeway.

The Oldest Road - an Exploration of the Ridgeway by J R L Anderson with photographs by Fay Godwin, Wildwood House, 1975. Paperback edition by Whittet Books, 1992.

The Ridgeway - a map guide by Footprint, revised edition 1994.

The Mountain Biker's Guide to the Ridgeway by Andy Bull and Frank Barrett, Stanley Paul & Co, 1991.

Walking in Britain, Lonely Planet, 2001 - includes a description of the western half of The Ridgeway.

Ridgeway Routes Pack - leaflets describing circular and other walks from The Ridgeway. Available from the National Trails Office.

Ridgeway Circular Riding Routes Pack - leaflets describing circular rides from The Ridgeway. Available from the National Trails Office.

Let's Hear it for The Ridgeway! by Elizabeth Newbery - a family activity book full of ideas and information on things to do and see on and close to The Ridgeway. Available from the National Trails Office.

Ridgeway Public Transport Leaflet - details of bus and train services for the whole Trail. Free from the National Trails Office.

Events Programme - a range of guided events around The Ridgeway. Free from the National Trails Office.

VII USEFUL CONTACTS

The Ridgeway Manager

Jos Joslin, National Trails Office, Cultural Services, Holton, Oxford OX33 1QQ. Telephone 01865 810224. Fax 01865 810207. Email: mail@rway-tpath.demon.co.uk

Highway Authorities responsible for public rights of way

Buckinghamshire County Council, Environmental Services Dept, County Hall, Walton Street, Aylesbury HP20 1UY. Telephone 01296 395000

Hertfordshire County Council, Planning and Environment, County Hall, Hertford SG13 8DN. Telephone 01992 555555

Oxfordshire County Council, Countryside Service, Cultural Services, Holton, Oxford OX33 1QQ. Telephone 01865 810226

Swindon Borough Council, Borough Engineer's Dept, Premier House, Station Road, Swindon SN1 1TZ. Telephone 01793 463000

West Berkshire Council, Countryside and Environment, Faraday Road, Newbury RG14 2AF. Telephone 01635 42400

Wiltshire County Council, Dept of Environmental Services, County Hall, Trowbridge, Wilts BA14 8JD. Telephone 01225 713000

Agency responsible for National Trails

Countryside Agency, South East and London Region, Dacre House, 19 Dacre Street, London SW1H 0DH. Telephone 0207 3402900

Organisations for walkers

Backpackers Club, c/o Jim & Maggie Beed, 49 Lyndhurst Road, Exmouth, Devon EX8 3DS. Telephone 01395 265159

Long Distance Walkers Association, c/o Les Maple, 21 Upcroft, Windsor SL4 3NH. Tel 01753 866685

Oxford Fieldpaths Society, c/o Mr D Godfrey, 23 Hawkswell House, Hawkswell Gardens, Oxford OX2 7EX. Tel 01865 514082

Ramblers Association, 2nd Floor, Camelford House, 87-89 Albert Embankment, London SE1 7TW 020 7339 8500

Code of Respect

To respect this National Trail so that it can be enjoyed by all, please . . .

Act responsibly to conserve The Ridgeway

Be aware and considerate of the rights of others

FOR RECREATION YOU CAN						
Use all The Ridgeway	walker					
Use all except footpath sections	cyclist, horserider					
Use all except footpath and bridleway sections	carriage driver, motorcyclist, four wheeled					

CODE OF RESPECT – YOU SHOULD						
Understand that others have legitimate access to many sections	walker, cyclist, horserider, carriage driver, motorcyclist, four wheeled, agricultural
Spread the message about responsible care	walker, cyclist, horserider, carriage driver, motorcyclist, four wheeled, agricultural
Follow the Country Code	walker, cyclist, horserider, carriage driver, motorcyclist, four wheeled, agricultural
Limit your use when the surface is vulnerable during and after wet weather	horserider, carriage driver, motorcyclist, four wheeled, agricultural
Avoid using The Ridgeway if you can find or develop another route	agricultural
Keep to well-used parts of the track to prevent damage to the whole width	motorcyclist, four wheeled, agricultural
Continue to help by reinstating the surface where possible	agricultural
Make sure you and your vehicle are fully road-legal	motorcyclist, four wheeled
Make sure your bicycle is roadworthy	cyclist
Drive at a quiet and careful speed with no more than 4 four-wheeled vehicles or 8 motorcycles in any one group	motorcyclist, four wheeled
Ride at a safe and controlled pace	cyclist, horserider
Help other users and make your own visit more enjoyable by using The Ridgeway when it is less busy	motorcyclist, four wheeled
Warn walkers of your approach and pass carefully	horserider, carriage driver
Warn walkers and horseriders of your approach and give way to them	cyclist
Give way to horseriders	walker, cyclist
Watch out for and respect temporary voluntary restraint signs and report registration numbers of those who break codes to LARA (Motoring Organisations' Land Access & Recreation Association). Tel: 01630 657627	motorcyclist, four wheeled

KEY

walker	carriage driver	driver - recreational four wheeled vehicle
cyclist	motorcyclist	
horserider		driver - agricultural vehicle

Organisations for cyclists

British Cycling Federation, National Cycling Centre, Stuart Street, Manchester M11 4DQ. Telephone 0870 8712000

Cyclists Touring Club (Off-Road), Cotterell House, 69 Meadrow, Godalming GU7 3HS. Telephone 01483 417217

Sustrans, 33 King Street, Bristol BS1 4DZ. Telephone 0117 9268893

Organisations for horseriders

British Horse Society, Stoneleigh Deer Park, Kenilworth CV8 2XZ. Telephone 01926 707700

Byways & Bridleways Trust, PO Box 117, Newcastle upon Tyne NE3 5YT. Telephone 0191 2364086

Endurance GB, National Agricultural Centre, Stoneleigh Park, Kenilworth CV8 2RP. Telephone 02476 698863

Other organisations

Berkshire, Buckinghamshire & Oxfordshire Wildlife Trust, The Lodge, 1 Armstrong Road, Littlemore, Oxford OX4 4XT. Telephone 01865 775476

Chiltern Society, The White Hill Centre, White Hill, Chesham, HP5 1AG. Telephone 01494 771250

Friends of the Ridgeway, c/o Mr Peter Gould, 18 Hampton Park, Bristol BS6 6LH.

Herts & Middlesex Wildlife Trust, Grebe House, St Michael's Street, St Albans AL3 4SN. Telephone 01727 858901

Wiltshire Wildlife Trust, Elm Tree Court, Long Street, Devizes, SN10 1NJ. Telephone 01380 725670

VIII GETTING THERE

Getting to The Ridgeway by public transport is fairly easy, particularly the eastern half of the Trail, and a useful map-based leaflet showing relevant public transport routes is available free from the National Trails Office (see page 16 for details).

Alternatively, telephone numbers and websites to find out more about public transport to the Trail are listed below:

• Rail Services   08457 484950 (24 hours a day)
                         www.railtrack.co.uk

• Bus Services   0870 6082608
                         www.pti.org.uk

Information about taxi services is included in each of the four sections.

Those wishing to travel to The Ridgeway by car are asked to park considerately if parking in villages on or close to the Trail. Other places to park are listed within each section.

Local Bus in Bishopstone

RESPECT THE COUNTRYSIDE IX

• Enjoy the countryside, but remember that most of The Ridgeway crosses private farmland and estates which are living and working landscapes.

• Always keep to the Trail to avoid trespass and use gates and stiles to negotiate fences and hedges.

• Crops and animals are the farmer's livelihood - please leave them alone.

• To avoid injury or distress to farm animals and wildlife, keep your dogs under close control at all times - preferably on a lead through fields with farm animals (NB if you are concerned that cattle are harassing you, it may be safer to let your dog off the lead).

• Remember to leave things as they are - fasten those gates you find closed. Straying farm animals can cause damage and inconvenience.

• Please take your litter home, otherwise it can injure people and animals and looks unsightly.

• Guard against all risk of fires especially in dry weather.

• Take special care on country roads and, if travelling by car, park sensibly so as not to obstruct others or gateways.

From Lodge Hill, southwest of Princes Risborough

X EMERGENCY CONTACTS

In emergency dial 999 and ask for the service required.

Police

To contact local police stations, telephone the number relevant to the section/county you are in and ask to be put through to the nearest police station.

Section	County	Tel Number
1	Wiltshire	01793 528111
	Oxfordshire	01865 846000
2	Oxfordshire & Berkshire	01865 846000
3	Oxfordshire	01865 846000
4	Oxfordshire & Buckinghamshire	01865 846000
	Hertfordshire	01707 354200

Grim's Ditch east of Wallingford during Spring

Hospitals

The following hospitals with casualty departments are located in the places shown below. The telephone numbers given are the hospital switchboard; ask to be put through to Accident and Emergency Reception.

◆ Full 24-hour emergency service

▼ Minor injuries only, 24-hour service

▲ Minor injuries only, NOT 24-hour service

Section	Town	Telephone No	Address
1	▼ Devizes	01380 723511	Devizes Community Hospital, Commercial Road, Devizes
	▲ Marlborough	01672 516631	Savernake Hospital, London Road, Marlborough (daily 8am-10pm)
	◆ Swindon	01793 536231	Princess Margaret Hospital, Okus Road, Swindon
2	▼ Wantage	01235 403801	Wantage Community Hospital, Garston Lane, Wantage
	▲ Didcot	01235 205860	Didcot Hospital, Wantage Road, Didcot (weekdays 6pm - 8am, weekends/bank hols 24 hrs)
3	▲ Wallingford	01491 208500	Wallingford Community Hospital, Reading Road, Wallingford (daily 9am-9pm)
4	◆ Aylesbury	01296 315000	Stoke Mandeville Hospital, Mandeville Road, Aylesbury

XI ACCOMMODATION, FACILITIES & SERVICES

This booklet gives details of the settlements, accommodation, eating places, shops, attractions and other facilities along The Ridgeway. They are listed in geographic order from Overton Hill to Ivinghoe Beacon.

If you fail to find accommodation using this guide please contact the Tourist Information Centres listed near the beginning of each section which may be able to provide other addresses.

The Ridgeway is divided into four sections as indicated on the map on page 5. At the start of each section is a map showing the settlements close to the Trail within that section. These maps are meant only as a guide and you are recommended to use this Companion in conjunction with The Ridgeway National Trail Guide or maps.

You are strongly advised to book accommodation in advance, and during summer as early as possible. Whilst booking, do check prices since those quoted here are usually the minimum charged.

For those who would like to enjoy more than a day on The Ridgeway without having to carry all their possessions, quite a few accommodation providers have indicated whether they are willing to transport the luggage you don't need during the day to your next night's accommodation. The fee charged for this service needs to be discussed and agreed at the time of the booking. Accommodation providers have also indicated if they are willing to collect you from The Ridgeway and deliver you back after your stay.

All the information within this Companion is as accurate as possible. Inclusion of accommodation does not constitute a recommendation although it is indicated in the details whether an establishment has a recognised grade awarded to it. If you have any comments or notice any errors, please write to Jos Joslin the National Trails Officer (page 16).

Camping on The Ridgeway

The situation regarding camping on The Ridgeway is, in theory, clear enough; The Ridgeway is privately owned and the public right of way along it is for passage only, not for stopping and camping.

In practice, however, most landowners do not object if a tent is pitched on The Ridgeway for a night and disappears the next morning as long as no litter is left, no damage done, nor camp fires lit. Do not camp in adjoining fields, woods or gallops without prior permission from the landowner.

Key to Symbols for Settlements

Any comments relate to preceding icon.

map grid reference (see start of each section for relevant maps)

shortest walking distance from The Ridgeway

most convenient train station

telephone

toilets

&WC   toilets adapted for disabled users

Tourist Information Centre

pub (usually open lunchtimes 11am-3pm then evenings 6pm-11pm)

bar meals in pub

post office (usual opening hours 9am-5.30pm weekdays; 9:00-12.30pm Sat)

general store (usual opening hours daily 9am-5.30pm Mon-Sat)

cafe/tea shop

restaurant

food take-away

opening hours of services relate to the preceding symbol

S M T W T F S

For example: open all day   open afternoon/evening

closed all day   open morning/lunchtime

£   bank (usually open daily 9.30am-4.30pm Mon-Fri)

cash machine available including outside bank opening hours

☆   tourist attraction

XI ACCOMMODATION, FACILITIES & SERVICES

Key to Symbols for Accommodation

Type of accommodation (symbols in margins)

A symbol in the margin indicates whether camping, youth hostel, self-catering or horse accommodation is available at that address - which may be in addition to bed and breakfast accommodation.

🔺 yha	youth hostel	INN	inn
⚑	camping	∪	grazing or stabling for horses
H	hotel		

Rose and Crown in Ashbury

Accommodation symbols

The number and price following the symbols for rooms gives the number and price of that type of room available. The same applies to tent/caravan pitches and stabling/grazing for horses. Prices quoted for rooms are the minimum price per room per night for bed and breakfast. The price for single occupancy of double, twin or family rooms is given in brackets eg (£22.00).

🛏	double room	💳	credit card(s) accepted
🛏	twin room	◆	English Tourism Council grade for B&Bs, guest houses, inns
🛏	family room		
🛏	single room	★	English Tourism Council grade for hotels
🚭	no smoking in bedrooms		
V	caters for vegetarians	▲	tent pitches
🍎	packed lunches available	🚐	caravan pitches
🍴	evening meals available at accommodation or locally	🚿	showers
		🚰	hot water
🐕	dogs allowed by arrangement	🚰	cold water
👫	children welcome	🚻	toilets
♿	wheelchair access	🧺	laundry facilities
DRY	clothes/boots drying facilities	🏪	site shop
🚗	transport to and from Trail by arrangement	(s)	stables
🧳	luggage transported to next overnight stop by arrangement	(g)	grazing for horses
🚲	secure cycle storage	⛏	special feature/comment

Uffington Castle

Avebury Stone Circle

Section 1

Overton Hill to Uffington Castle

Probably the most remote section of The Ridgeway, this 35 km
(22 miles) stretch of broad track runs along the ridge of chalk
downland in Wiltshire and Oxfordshire. It passes through an
immensely rich area of archaeology and past the only pub
directly on the western half of the Trail!

(Not to scale)

A Taster

In places you can feel on top of the world with undulating downland and dry valleys or combes to the south and the Thames Valley stretching away northwards to the Cotswolds in the far distance. A characteristic sight from Overton Hill to Barbury Castle is small clumps of beech woodland planted by the Victorians as landscape features and to give sheep some shelter. Some clumps are even planted on top of Bronze Age round barrows, frowned upon today because of the damage tree roots do to ancient monuments.

The countryside is a mixture of arable land, which changes colour with the seasons, and areas of sheep or cattle grazed grassland. Some of the best views are from Smeathe's Ridge between Barbury Castle and Ogbourne St George.

The villages of Ogbourne St George in the valley of the River Og and those at the foot of the downs such as Bishopstone, Ashbury and Woolstone contain many lovely cottages some of them built out of blocks of chalk with thatched roofs.

This section includes a crossing by bridge of the M4, but the motorway only intrudes upon your journey for a short while and is soon lost as you climb away from it.

Bishopstone

History

This section starts in what is probably the richest area of archaeology in Britain, the World Heritage Site of Avebury. Within 2 km (1.2 miles) of the start at Overton Hill you can reach the Avebury Stone Circle, Silbury Hill (the largest man-made mound in Europe constructed by Stone Age people using antler picks and shovels made from the shoulder blades of oxen), West Kennett long barrow, the Sanctuary, the Stone Avenue and Fyfield Down National Nature Reserve littered with sarsen stones.

Travelling north, below you at Hackpen Hill you pass the first of the hill figures cut into the chalk which are scattered along the length of The Ridgeway. The Hackpen White Horse was created in 1838 by a local parish clerk. A little further on you reach the first of three Iron Age forts found in this section, Barbury Castle. Unlike the other two, Liddington Castle and Uffington Castle, both of which The Ridgeway skirts, you pass right through the centre of this fort.

Just northeast of Ogbourne St George and to the east of The Ridgeway lies the deserted village of Snap abandoned early this century as a result of agricultural depression. With records dating from 1268, by 1841 Snap was a thriving if small farming community of 47 people. However, cheap corn from America in the 1870s caused the rapid decline in the population and the village's final demise. Today just low piles of sarsen rubble marking the site of cottages remain visible during winter months.

Before you reach Uffington Castle, away to the south is the delightful 17th century Ashdown House set in a tremendous remote dry valley location and the fine Wayland's Smithy long barrow just 50 m north of your route.

Maps		
Landranger maps	173	Swindon and Devizes
	174	Newbury and Wantage
Explorer maps	157	Marlborough and Savernake Forest
	170	Abingdon, Wantage and Vale of White Horse

Public Transport Information

Rail Services   08457 484950 (24 hours a day)
www.railtrack.co.uk

Bus Services   0870 6082608
www.pti.org.uk

Taxis

Place	Name	Telephone Number
Marlborough	Marlborough Taxis	01672 512786
	Arrow Private Hire	01672 515567
Swindon	Swindon Black Cabs	01793 535354/0800 654321
	United Cars	01793 611111
	Millennium Radio Cars	01793 610000/513333
Lambourn	Ray's Taxis	01488 71819

Car Parking

The following are places close to or on The Ridgeway, other than villages or towns, with parking for vehicles - at some only for a few. Unfortunately theft from vehicles parked in the countryside does occasionally occur, so please leave valuables at home.

Place	Map Grid Reference
On Ridgeway at the start at Overton Hill, on north side of A4, 7 km (4.5 miles) west of Marlborough	SU 119681
On Ridgeway at Hackpen Hill on minor road between Marlborough and Broad Hinton, 3 km (2 miles) east of Broad Hinton	SU 129747
On Ridgeway at Barbury Castle Country Park, 8 km (5 miles) south of Swindon signed from Wroughton and Chiseldon	SU 157762

Place	Map Grid Reference
On Ridgeway at Fox Hill near Wanborough, 200m northeast of Shepherds Rest pub on road to Hinton Parva	SU 233814
On Ridgeway 1 km (0.5 miles) south of Ashbury on B4000	SU 274844
National Trust car park for Uffington White Horse, south off B4507, 700m (0.5 miles) north of The Ridgeway	SU 293866

Water Taps

- with troughs for animals

Place	Map Grid Reference
Barbury Castle Country Park (at the bungalow)	SU 158760
Elm Tree Cottage, Southend	SU 198734
• Idstone Barn, Ashbury	SU 263835

Toilets

Place	Map Grid Reference
Barbury Castle Country Park	SU 155762
Shepherds Rest Pub, Fox Hill (patrons only)	SU 232813

Police

Wiltshire	01793 528111
Oxfordshire	01865 846000

Hospitals

Place	Telephone Number	Address
Devizes	01380 723511	Devizes Community Hospital, Commercial Road, Devizes
Marlborough	01672 516631	Savernake Hospital, London Road, Marlborough (daily 8am-10pm)
Swindon	01793 536231	Princess Margaret Hospital, Okus Road, Swindon

Vets

Place	Name		Telephone Number
Marlborough	Holden & Reader		01672 512043
	Hayward & Sercombe		01672 514875
Wroughton	Archway		01793 812542
Swindon	Drove Veterinary Hospital		01793 522483/523705
	Arrow Veterinary Group		01793 832461
	Lawn Veterinary Hospital		01793 644422
Lambourn	Hall and Lawrence		01488 73755
	Ridgeway Group	Equine	01488 71999
		Small animals	01488 71505
Faringdon	Danetree		01367 242777
	Elms Surgery		01367 242416

Farriers

Place	Name	Telephone Number
Marlborough	Baker	01672 514013
Aldbourne	Racing Farriers	01672 540812
Swindon	P J Groom	01793 644123
Wroughton	P A Groom	01793 814185
Shrivenham	T P Morrissey	01793 783581
Lambourn	Mr Alderton	07831 594442
	Charles	01488 71310 or 07831 595073
	Pickford	01488 72613

34

Saddlers

Place	Name	Telephone Number
Purton (near Swindon)	Elmgrove Saddlery	01793 770613
Highworth	The Saddlery	01793 766660
Lambourn	Wicks	01488 71766
Faringdon	S and J M Cooper	01367 240517

Mountain Bike Hire

Place	Name	Telephone Number
Swindon	Swindon Cycles	01793 700105
	Express Cycles	0800 018 29253

Bike Repairs

Place	Name	Telephone Number
Swindon	Mitchell Cycles	01793 523306
	Swindon Cycles	01793 700105
	Bike Doctor	01793 874873
	Express Cycles	0800 01829253
	Total Fitness	01793 644185

Cottage in Ashbury

Racehorses during morning exercise

Tourist Information Centres

★ offers accommodation booking service

Place	Address/Opening Hours
Avebury	Opening 2002 Tel Devizes Tourist Information Centre 01380 729408 for details

★ Marlborough George Lane Car Park, Marlborough SN8 1EE,
Tel/Fax: 01672 513989

Opening hours:
Summer (Apr-Oct) Mon-Sat 10:00-17:00
Winter (Nov-Mar) Mon-Sat 10:00-16:30

★ Swindon 37 Regent Street, Swindon SN1 1JL
Tel: 01793 530328 Fax: 01793 434031

Opening hours: All year: Mon-Sat 09:15-17:00

★ Faringdon 7a Market Place, Faringdon SN7 7HL Tel/Fax: 01367 242191

Opening hours:
Summer (1 Apr-31 Oct) Mon-Fri 10:00-17:00, Sat 10:00-13:00
Winter (1 Nov-31 Mar) Mon-Sat 10:00-13:00

Ashdown House 4 km south of Ashbury

Marlborough

 SU1969 🏠 7km (4.4 miles)

Market town with range of services

🚂 Swindon 18km (11 miles) 🛈

Browns Farm

Marlborough, Wilts
Tel 01672 515129

Peaceful farmhouse set on the edge of Savernake Forest.

Tea/coffee facilities, some with en-suite facilities. Ideal base for touring Wiltshire. Immediate access to footpaths & bridleways. Working Dairy/Arable Farm. TV Lounge and large gardens available for guests. Ample off-street parking

---

| **Browns Farm** | *all year* | 🌙 |

☀ SU198678 1.5km(0.9miles) south of Marlborough

Mrs Hazel Crockford

Browns Farm, MARLBOROUGH, Wilts SN8 4ND

☎ 01672 515129 **Mob:** 07931 311985

Email: crockford@farming.co.uk

🛏 2 🛏 1 🛏 1 £34.00 (£20.00) 🚭

 V 🏔 🔲 🚻 **DRY** 🚲

 Mastercard, Visa

Ⓢ 2 £10.00 Ⓖ 4 £10.00

West Overton

 SU1368 🏠 1km (0.6 miles)

🚂 Swindon 21km (13 miles) 📞

| 🍺 | S M T W T F S | ✕ | S M T W T F S |
| 🧺 | S M T W T F S | | |

| **Cairncot** | *all year* |

Mrs Rachel Leigh

Cairncot, West Overton, MARLBOROUGH, Wilts SN8 4ER

☎ 01672 861617 **Mob:** 07798 603455

🛏 1 £40.00 (£30.00) 🛏 1 £20.00 🚭

 V 🏔 🔲 🚻 🚭 **DRY** 🚗 🦽 🚲 ♦♦♦

Avebury

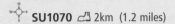 **SU1070** 🥾 2km (1.2 miles)

🚂 Swindon 20km (12 miles) 📞 ♿WC ℹ️

☆ Avebury World Heritage Site,
website: www.avebury.demon.co.uk
Alexander Keiller Museum tel: 01672
539250

Manor Farm	*all year*

Mrs J Farthing
Manor Farm, High Street, Avebury,
MARLBOROUGH, Wilts SN8 1RF
☎ 01672 539294 **Fax:** 01672 539294

🛏 1 🛏 1 £57.00 (£40.00) 🚭 V 🧺
👫 over 12 years 🚲 ◆◆◆◆

Manor Farm	*closed Nov - Mar*

⚑ SU097087 500m west of Avebury
Mrs Julia Butler
Manor Farm, Avebury Trusloe,
MARLBOROUGH, Wilts SN8 1QY
☎ 01672 539243

🛏 1 £48.00 (£38.00) 🚭 🚲 ◆◆◆

Winterbourne Monkton

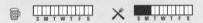 **SU1072** 🥾 3km (1.9 miles)

🚂 Swindon 15km (9 miles) 📞

Winterbourne Bassett

 **SU1075** 🥾 3km (1.9 miles)

🚂 Swindon 13km (8 miles) 📞

Broad Hinton

SU1076 🥾 3km (1.9 miles)

🚂 Swindon 11km (7 miles) 📞

Barbury Castle

SU1576 on The Ridgeway

🚂 Swindon 10km (6 miles) 📞 ⚙

☆ Barbury Castle Country Park tel: 01793
771419

Smeathe's Ridge

Barbury Castle from the west

Villiers Inn

Wroughton, Oxfordshire

Tel: **01793 814744**   *Fax:* **01793 814119**

In 1870 Moormead Farm always ensured that its residents were comfortable, well fed and watered.

Nowadays it is Villiers Inn and the objectives remain the same. Villiers Inn aims to provide exceptional value for money whilst avoiding the dreary monotony that is so typical of the economy hotel genre.

Instead Villiers Inn is a warm-hearted, full-service hotel with personality!

Wroughton

SU1480 4km (2.5 miles)

Swindon 5km (3 miles) ☎ ♿WC

	S M T W T F S		S M T W T F S
🍺		✖	
✉		🧺	
☕		🎴	
🏧			

£ Inside Coventry Newsagent
☆ Science Museum tel: 01793 814466

H | Villiers Inn   *all year*

The Manager
Villiers Inn, Moormead Road, Wroughton,
SWINDON, Wilts SN4 9BY
☎ 01793 814744 **Fax:** 01793 814119
Email: hotels@villiersinn.co.uk
Website: www.villiersinn.co.uk

🛏 18 🛏 11 £69.00 (£49.00)
🛏 4 £49.00 **V** 🔥🚭🅿🛠🚻♿ **DRY**
🚗 🐾 🚲 💳 Mastercard, Visa,
American Express, Delta ★ ★ ★

Swindon

SU1583 9km (5.6 miles)
Large town with range of services

Swindon ℹ

☆ Oasis Leisure Centre tel: 01793 445400.
Coate Water Country Park tel: 01793 490150.
Great Western Railway Museum & Railway
Village Museum tel: 01793 466555

Chiseldon

SU1879 3km (1.9 miles)

Swindon 8km (5 miles) ☎

	S M T W T F S		S M T W T F S
🍺		✖	
✉		🧺	

Courtleigh House   *all year*

Mrs Ruth Hibberd
Courtleigh House, 40 Draycott Road,
Chiseldon, SWINDON, Wilts SN4 0LS
☎ 01793 740246

🛏 2 £40.00 (£22.00) 🛏 1 £22.00 🚭
🛠 **DRY** 🚗 🚲 ◆◆◆◆

Ogbourne St George

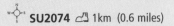 SU2074 ⌂ 1km (0.6 miles)

🚆 Swindon 13km (8 miles) 📞

🍺 [SMTWTFS] ✕ [SMTWTFS]

🏕 Foxlynch *all year*

Mr G Edwins
Foxlynch, Ogbourne St George,
MARLBOROUGH, Wilts SN8 1TD
☎ 01672 841307

🛏 1 £15/person (£15.00) 🛏 2 £15.00
🚭 📶 ✝ DRY 🚗 ☂ 🚲
🛏 Family bunkroom in stable block

⛺ 4 £4/person 🚐 1 £4/person 📱 ♿ 🚶 ⓦ

ⓢ 4 £8.50

🅗 Parklands Hotel *all year*

Mr Mark Bentley
Parklands Hotel, High Street, Ogbourne St
George, MARLBOROUGH, Wilts SN8 1SL
☎ 01672 841555 **Fax:** 01672 841533
Email: enquiries@parklandshoteluk.co.uk
Website: www.parklandshoteluk.co.uk

🛏 2 🛏 6 £60.00 (£50.00)
🛏 2 £45.00 🚭 V 🚶 🌙 📶 ✝ DRY 🚶
🚲 💳 Mastercard, Visa, Delta, Switch,
Solo ♦♦♦♦
🛏 All rooms en-suite

The Old Crown *all year* 🏨

Mr & Mrs Megan & Michael Shaw
The Old Crown, Marlborough Road,
Ogbourne St George, MARLBOROUGH,
Wilts SN8 1SL
☎ 01672 841445 **Fax:** 01672 841056
Email:
theinnwiththewell@compuserve.com
Website: www.theinnwiththewell.com

🛏 2 🛏 3 🛏 1 £45.00 (£40.00)
🚭 V 🚶 🌙 Except Sundays 📶 ✝ ♿
DRY 🚲 💳 Mastercard, Visa, American
Express, Delta

Liddington

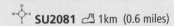 SU2081 ⌂ 1km (0.6 miles)

🚆 Swindon 7km (4 miles) 📞

🍺 [SMTWTFS] ✕ [SMTWTFS]
✉ [SMTWTFS] 🧺 [SMTWTFS]

☆ Liddington Castle

Street House Farm *closed Xmas*

Mrs Elizabeth Dixon
Street House Farm, Liddington, SWINDON,
Wilts SN4 0HD
☎ 01793 790243

🛏 1 🛏 1 £40.00 (£22.00) 🚭 V 🚶
📶 ✝ DRY 🚗 🚶 🚲

The Old Crown

"The Inn with the Well"

Ogbourne St George, Wilts
☎ **01672 841445**
Fax 01672 841056
www.theinnwiththewell.com

Traditional Inn with acclaimed
Restaurant (non smoking)
Rooms built 2000 - all ensuite with TV,
hospitality tray, hairdryer and duck!

Food served on all sessions.
Closed Sunday evenings &
Monday lunchtimes

Wanborough

 SU2182 🛏 2km (1.2 miles)

🚂 Swindon 7km (4 miles)

Iris Cottage   *closed Xmas*

Mrs Joan Rosier
Iris Cottage, Burycroft, Lower
Wanborough, SWINDON, Wilts SN4 0AP
☎ 01793 790591

🛏 1 £40.00 (£22.00)   🛏 2 £22.00

The Shepherds Rest   *all year*

⌖ SU231813 on The Ridgeway
Mr M Harold
The Shepherds Rest, Foxhill, Wanborough,
SWINDON, Wilts SN4 0DR
☎ 01793 790266 **Fax:** 01793 790353

Å 6 £POA 🔲 DRY 🔲 🔲 🔲 🔲 🔲

View from The Ridgeway near Liddington Castle

Bishopstone

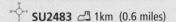

SU2483 1km (0.6 miles)

Swindon 11km (7 miles)

S M T W T F S   ✕   S M T W T F S

Cheney Thatch   *closed Xmas, New Year*

Mrs Rosemary Boot
Cheney Thatch, Oxon Lane, Bishopstone,
SWINDON, Wilts SN6 8PS
☎ 01793 790508

2 £40.00 (£25.00)
over 10 years

Royal Oak   *all year*   INN

Mr Brian Walkley
The Royal Oak, Cues Lane, Bishopstone Nr
SWINDON, Wilts SN6 8PP
☎ 01793 790481 **Mob:** 07949 010238
Fax: 01793 790481
Email:royaloak_bishopstone@lineone.net
Website: www.arkells.com/royaloak-bishopstone/index.htm

1   1   2 £40.00 (£30.00)
V
Mastercard, Visa, Delta, other

Cheney Thatch

Bishopstone, Swindon, Wiltshire   ☎ **01793 790508**

16th Century stone thatched cottage in unique peaceful setting. Trout stream through garden, summer marquee. Heated outdoor swimming pool. Footpath to Ridgeway from garden gate.

The Royal Oak

Bishopstone, Wilts
☎ **01793 790481**
**www.arkells.com/royaloak-
bishopstone/index/htm**

Bishopstone is a pretty village 3/4 mile
from The Ridgeway National Trail.

A warm welcome awaits you at
The Oak. In winter a log fire.
A la carte menu serving freshly cooked
organic food every day.

Marquee available for the bigger
occasion.

Prebendal Farm *closed Xmas, New Year*

Mrs Jo Selbourne
Prebendal Farm, Bishopstone, SWINDON,
Wilts SN6 8PT
☎ 01793 790485 **Fax:** 01793 791487
Email: prebendal@aol.com

🛏3 🛏1 £50.00 (£25.00) 🛏1 £25.00
V 🖾🖼 🛉🛉 DRY 🚗 🛉🛉 🚲

Ashbury

📍 **SU2685** 🥾 1km (0.6 miles)

🍺 Swindon 13km (8 miles)

🍴	S M T W T F S
🍽	S M T W T F S
✉	S M T W T F S
🛒	S M T W T F S

☆ Ashdown House tel: 01488 725584

Rose & Crown Hotel *all year* Ⓗ

Ms June Blake
Rose & Crown Hotel, High Street, Ashbury,
SWINDON, Wilts SN6 8NA
☎ 01793 710222 **Fax:** 01793 710029
Email: juneblake@bt.com

🛏 5 🛏 4 🛏 1 £60.00 (£45.00)
🛏 1 £45.00 🚫 V 🖾🖼 🛉🛉 ♿ DRY 🚗
🛉🛉 🚲 💳 Mastercard, Visa, American
Express, Delta, other

Woolstone

 SU2987 2km (1.2 miles)

Swindon 18km (11 miles)

Hickory House   *closed Xmas, New Year*

Mrs Caroline Grist
Hickory House, Woolstone, FARINGDON,
Oxon SN7 7QL
☎ 01367 820303 **Fax:** 01367 820958
Email: rlg@hickoryhouse.freeserve.co.uk
Website: www.stilwell.co.uk

2 £38.00 (£25.00) V
over 12 years DRY

The White Horse   *all year* INN

Mrs Maureen Batty
The White Horse, Woolstone, FARINGDON,
Oxon SN7 7QL
☎ 01367 820726 **Fax:** 01367 820566
Email: uffingtonwhorse@aol.com
Website:
www.whitehorseuffington.co.uk

4 2 1 £65.00 (£50.00)
V DRY
Mastercard, Visa, American Express, Delta
◆◆◆◆

Tel:
01367
820303

Fax:
01367
820958

Hickory House

Hickory House, Woolstone, Oxfordshire

Comfortable en-suite bedrooms in self-contained extension in beautiful village.
Pub serving food is two minutes walk from the house.

THE WHITE HORSE

Woolstone, Oxfordshire

Tel: **01367 820726**   *Fax:* **01367 820566**

**16th Century inn situated under 'Uffington White Horse'
in lovely olde world village of Woolstone.**

All rooms en-suite with Sky TV. Hospitality trays, hairdryers etc.

In winter enjoy our log fires and in summer our lovely garden.
We pride ourselves on serving freshly cooked local produce.
A la carte reataurant and bar meals.

Uffington

✦ **SU3089** 🏠 3km (1.9 miles)

🚆 Swindon 19km (12 miles) 📞 ♿

🍺 | S M T W T F S   ✕ | S M T W T F S

✉ | S M T W T F S   🧺 | S M T W T F S

🫖 | S M T W T F S

☆ Tom Browns School Museum
tel: 01367 820259

⛺ Britchcombe Farm   *all year*

✦ SU307872 1km (0.6 miles) from
Ridgeway

Mrs M Seymour

Britchcombe Farm, Uffington, FARINGDON,
Oxon SN7 7QJ

☎ 01367 820667 **Mob:** 07748 005362

⛺ 20 £3/person 🚐 10 £3/person 🚭
🔥 📶 ♀♂ **DRY** 🚗 🚲 📺 ♨ 🐕 ♿
🛏 Mobile homes from £100 per week

Norton House   *all year*

Mrs Fenella Oberman

Norton House, Broad Street, Uffington,
FARINGDON, Oxon SN7 7RA

☎ 01367 820230 **Fax:** 01367 820230

Email: carloberman@cs.com

🛏 1 🛏 1 🛏 1 £40.00 (£25.00)
🛏 1 £22.00 🚭 V 🔥 📶 ♀♂ **DRY** 🚗
♿ 🚲

Sower Hill Farm   *all year*

✦ SU307872 1km (0.6 miles) from
Ridgeway

Mrs Sylvia Cox

Sower Hill Farm, Uffington, FARINGDON,
Oxon SN7 7QH

☎ 01367 820758

🛏 1 🛏 1 £40.00 (£25.00)
🛏 1 £20.00 🚭 V 🔥 **DRY** ♿ 🚲

Faringdon

✦ **SU2895** 🏠 9.5km (6 miles)

Town with range of services

🚆 Swindon 18km (11 miles) ℹ

Sudbury House Hotel   *all year* Ⓗ

Mr Andrew Ibbotson

Sudbury House Hotel, Folly Hill,
FARINGDON, Oxon SN7 8AA

☎ 01367 241272 **Fax:** 01367 242346

Email: stay@sudburyhouse.co.uk

Website: www.sudburyhouse.co.uk

🛏 39 🛏 10 🛏 3 £70.00 (£60.00)
V 🔥 🚭 📶 ♀♂ ♿ **DRY** ♿ 🚲
 Mastercard, Visa, American Express,
Delta, Other ★ ★ ★
🛏 Smoking permitted in certain rooms
only

Section 2

Uffington Castle to Streatley

This 33 km (21 miles) stretch of The Ridgeway keeps to the high
scarp edge of the open downland in Oxfordshire and Berkshire
and includes the widest parts of the Trail and some of the best
conditions underfoot. There's also lots of history to explore.

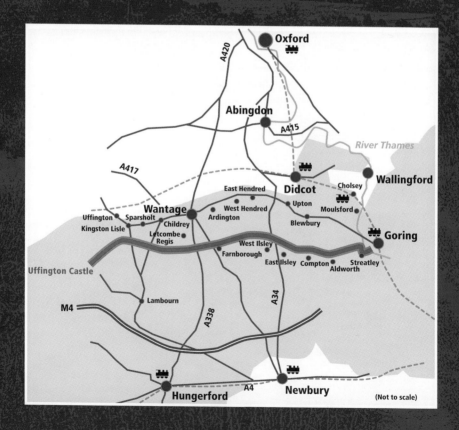

A Taster

Rolling open downland to the south, punctuated in places by small woodlands, and fine views north into the Vale of White Horse and the Thames Valley are typical of this section. On a clear day you can see the hills in the distance behind which nestles Oxford and, further east, the Chiltern Hills through which The Ridgeway later travels. Dominating the view from many places are the cooling towers of Didcot power station just 10 km (6 miles) north, sometimes menacing and inappropriate but at other times strangely beautiful.

This is horse racing country and an early riser will encounter strings of racehorses exercising on the numerous gallops, long ribbons of well managed grass tracks, adjacent to The Ridgeway. The turf of the downland drains easily through the chalk just below creating excellent going for horses.

Small villages are strung out below to the north at the spring line where water seeps between different geological layers. Many of these are worth a visit to enjoy the local vernacular architecture which includes cottages built from chalk blocks quarried from the downs.

This section also negotiates the A34 north-south trunk road by an underpass. The noise of the traffic is counteracted to some extent by the colourful mural depicting local historical scenes painted by local people on the walls of the underpass.

Uffington Manger

History

This section is steeped in history from prehistoric times right through to this century. The earliest monuments are the round barrows, burial chambers dating from Bronze Age times, roughly from 2000 to 750 BC. There are several close to The Ridgeway, including one in the area of woodland at Scutchamer's Knob above East Hendred which was excavated and ruthlessly dug away in 1842. Another lies within the width of the path a kilometre west of the B4494 road.

Two Iron Age forts grace this part of The Ridgeway, Uffington Castle and Segsbury Camp. Just a short distance from the former lies the most famous hill figure in the country, the Uffington White Horse, and below this Dragon Hill, a natural mound where, reputedly, St George killed his dragon. The bare chalk patch on the top is said to be where the blood of the dragon was spilt and no grass will now grow.

The Saxons have left their mark in this area with Wantage being the birth place of King Alfred who subsequently fought battles on the downs. Wantage also gave its name to Lord Wantage whose wife erected the monument to her husband on The Ridgeway just east of the B4494. His descendants still own the model farm and villages he built at the end of the last century.

A little further east of here and to the south lies the village of East Ilsley famous for its sheep fairs which only finished in the 1930s.

**Statue of King Alfred
in Wantage Market Place**

Maps

| Landranger maps | 174 | Newbury and Wantage |
| Explorer maps | 170 | Abingdon, Wantage and Vale of White Horse |

Public Transport Information

Rail Services	08457 484950 (24 hours a day)
	www.railtrack.co.uk
Bus Services	0870 6082608
	www.pti.org.uk

Taxis

Place	Name	Telephone Number
Lambourn	Ray's Taxis	01488 71819
East Challow	Laser Cars	01235 762647/07973 627051
	Stuart's Taxis	01235 770608
Denchworth	Sapphire Cabs	01235 771212/772424
Wantage	Gemini Cars	0800 0282219
Grove (near Wantage)	Grove Cabs	01235 772200
	Evenload Taxis	01235 762035
Chilton	Rural Carriages	01235 834469
Compton	Compton Passenger Service	01635 579076
Blewbury	Rural Connections	01235 851010
Didcot	Bob's	01235 512121
	Harold's	01235 512345
	Pryor's	01235 812345
	Zodiac Cars	07074 201747
Goring	Murdock's Taxi Service	01491 872029
	M & S Taxis	01491 873253

Car Parking

The following are places close to or on The Ridgeway, other than villages or towns, with parking for vehicles - at some only for a few. Unfortunately theft from vehicles parked in the countryside does occasionally occur so please leave valuables at home.

Place	Map Grid Reference
National Trust car park for Uffington White Horse, south off B4507, 700m (0.5 miles) north of The Ridgeway	SU 293866
On Ridgeway at Sparsholt Firs on the south side of the B4001, 4km (2.5 miles) south of Childrey	SU 344851
On Ridgeway on the east side of B4494, 5km (3 miles) south of Wantage	SU 417843
On Ridgeway at Scutchamer's Knob, 3km (2 miles) south of E Hendred off the A417 east of wantage	SU 458851
On Ridgeway at Bury Down on minor road from A34 to W Ilsley (signed Ridgeway from A34)	SU 479841
On Ridgeway at end of Rectory Road, Streatley west off A417	SU 567813

Blewbury Down north of Compton

Water Taps

- with troughs for animals

Place	Map Grid Reference
Hill Barn Sparsholt	SU 338854
The Ridgeway Youth Hostel, Letcombe Regis	SU 393849
Compton Down	SU 506823

Toilets

The Ridgeway Youth Hostel, Letcombe Regis   SU 393849

Police

Oxfordshire and Berkshire   01865 846000

Hospitals

Place	Telephone Number	Name
Swindon	01793 536231	Princess Margaret Hospital, Okus Road, Swindon
Wantage	01235 403801	Wantage Community Hospital, Garston Lane, Wantage
Didcot	01235 517900	Didcot Hospital, Wantage Road, Didcot. (weekdays 6pm - 8am, weekends/bank holidays 24 hours)

Vets

Place	Name		Telephone Number
Lambourn	Hall and Lawrence		01488 73755
	Ridgeway Group	Equine	01488 71999
		Small animals	01488 71505
Faringdon	Danetree		01367 242777
	Elms Surgery		01367 242416
Wantage	Abivale Group		01235 770333
	Danetree		01235 770227
West Ilsley	Clemenger		01635 281344

Place	Name	Telphone Number
Didcot	Abivale Group	01235 511553
	Larkmead Group	01235 814991
	Hadden Hill Veterinary Centre	01235 511553
Cholsey	Larkmead Group	01491 651479

Farriers

Place	Name	Telphone Number
Lambourn	Mr Alderton	017831 594442
	Charles	01488 71310/07831 595073
	Pickford	01488 72613

Saddlers

Place	Name	Telphone Number
Lambourn	Wicks	01488 71766
Faringdon	S & J M Cooper	01367 240517
Goosey		
(near Faringdon)	Asti Stud Saddlery	01367 710288
Denchworth	Denchworth Equestrian	
(near Wantage)	Supplies	01235 868175
Blewbury	Arena Saddlery	01235 850725/07702 685072

Mountain Bike Hire

Place	Name	Telphone Number
Abingdon	Pedal power	01235 525123

Bike Repairs

Place	Name	Telphone Number
Wantage	Ridgeway Cycles	01235 764445
	GMC	01235 764204
Didcot	Dentons	01235 816566
Abingdon	Braggs	01235 520034
	Pedal power	01235 525123
	Behind Bars	01235 535624

Tourist Information Centres

★ offers accommodation booking service

Place	Address/Opening Hours
★ Faringdon	7a Market Place, Faringdon SN7 7HL Tel/Fax: 01367 242191 Opening hours: Summer (1 Apr-31 Oct) Mon-Fri 10:00-17:00, Sat 10:00-13:00 Winter (1 Nov-31 Mar) Mon-Sat 10:00-13:00
★ Wantage	19 Church Street, Wantage OX12 8BL Tel/Fax: 01235 760176 Opening hours: All year: Mon-Sat 10:30-16:30, Sun 14:30-17.00
★ Abingdon	25 Bridge Street, Abingdon OX14 3HN Tel: 01235 522711 Fax: 01235 535245 Opening hours: Summer (1 Apr-31 Oct) Mon-Sat 10:00-17:00 Winter (1 Nov-31 Mar) Mon-Fri 10:00-16:00, Sat 09:30-14:30
★ Didcot	Station Road Car Park, Didcot OX11 7NR Tel/Fax: 01235 813243 Opening hours: Summer (Jul-Aug) Mon-Sat 10:00-17:00, Sun 10:00-16:00 Winter (Sep-Jun) Mon-Sat 10:00-16:00

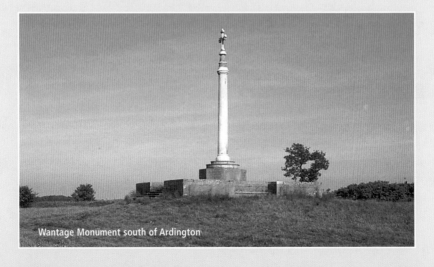

Wantage Monument south of Ardington

Kingston Lisle

⌖ **SU3287** 🛏 2km (1.2 miles)

🚂 Swindon 22km (14 miles) 📞

🍺 ▮▮▯▯▯▯▯ S M T W T F S ✕ ▮▮▯▯▯▯▯ S M T W T F S

Down Barn Farm

Down Barn Farm, Sparsholt, Wantage, Oxfordshire.

Down Barn Farm stands in complete isolation and total peace and quiet in a hollow of the downs $\frac{1}{4}$ mile from The Ridgeway. It is a working farm producing organic beef and pork. Horses are trained for Endurance Riding.

Tel: **01367 820272**
Mobile: **0777 5678244**

Sparsholt

⌖ **SU3487** 🛏 3km (1.9 miles)

🚂 Didcot 20km (12 miles) 📞

🍺 ▯▯▯▯▯▯▯ S M T W T F S ✕ ▮▮▯▯▯▯▯ S M T W T F S

| Down Barn Farm | phone ahead | |

⌖ SU333852 2km 600m south of the Ridgeway

Mrs Penny Reid
Down Barn Farm, Sparsholt Down,
WANTAGE, Oxon OX12 9XD
☎ 01367 820272
Email: pendomeffect@aol.com

🛏 1 🛏 2 £40.00 (£25.00) 🚫 V 🏃
🍴 except Sundays 🔖 ⚥ ♿ **DRY** 🚗
🚶 🚲

⛺ 4 £5.00 🚐 1 £10.00 📖 ♨ ⚡ ⚥ ⬚

Ⓢ 4 £8.00 Ⓖ 6 £5.00

Spindle

Westcot Lodge · *closed Xmas & Easter*

-✧- SU339874 2km (1.2miles) from Ridgeway

Mrs P Upton
Westcot Lodge, Westcot, Sparsholt, WANTAGE, Oxon OX12 9QA
☎ 01235 751251 **Mob:** 07730 124888
Fax: 01235 751251

🛏 1 🛏 1 £60.00 (£60.00)
🛏 1 £30.00 🚭 V 🌿 🔥 🕺 DRY 🚗
🦽 🚲

INN | The Star Inn · *all year*

Mr A J Fowles
The Star Inn, Watery Lane, SPARSHOLT, Oxon OX12 9PL
☎ 01235 751001 **Fax:** 01235 751539
Email: star.inn@amserve.net

🛏 2 🛏 5 🛏 1 £60.00 (£60.00) 🚭
V 🔥 🕺 ♿ 💳 Mastercard, Visa, Delta,
Switch ◆◆◆◆
🍴 Extra charge for breakfast from £5.00

Childrey

-✧- **SU3687** 🚶 4km (2.5 miles)

🚂 Didcot 18km (11 miles) 📞

  ✕
✉ 🧺

Letcombe Regis

-✧- **SU3886** 🚶 2km (1.2 miles)

🚂 Didcot 16km (10 miles) 📞

🍺  ✕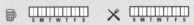

YHA Ridgeway Centre · *phone ahead*

-✧- SU393849 600m from Ridgeway

The Manager
YHA Ridgeway Centre, Court Hill, Letcombe Regis, WANTAGE, Oxon OX12 9NE
☎ 01235 760253 **Fax:** 01235 768865

🚭 V 🌿 🔥 🕺 ♿ DRY 🚲
🍴 Dormitory accommodation £10.25/adult

🏕 many £5.15 🔥 ♿ 🚿 ☺ 🔌

ⓢ 4 £9.00

Quince Cottage · *all year*

Mrs Louise Boden
Quince Cottage, Letcombe Regis, WANTAGE, Oxon OX12 9JP
☎ 01235 763652
Email: bodens@supanet.com

🛏 1 🛏 1 £45 - 55 (£26.00) 🚭
V 🌿 🕺 DRY 🚲

Regis B & B *all year*

Mrs Millie Rastall
Regis B & B, 2 Court Road, Letcombe
Regis, WANTAGE, Oxon OX12 9JH
☎ 01235 762860 **Mob:** 07713 880 457
Fax: 01235 769975
Email: millierastall@aol.com

🛏 2 🛏 1 £45.00 (£28.00) 🛏 1 £23.00
🚭 V 🐾 🚫 ♿ **DRY** 🚗 🚶 🚲

The Old Vicarage *all year*

Mrs G F Barton
The Old Vicarage, Letcombe Regis,
WANTAGE, Oxon OX12 9JP
☎ 01235 765827
Email: hugh.barton@queensclub.co.uk

🛏 2 🛏 1 £45.00 (£30.00) 🛏 1 £25.00
🚭 V 🐾 ♿ **DRY** 🚗 🚶 🚲

The Old Vicarage

Letcombe Regis, Wantage, Oxfordshire

Tel/Fax: **01235 765827**

A substantial Victorian vicarage set in a
delightful garden offering comfortable
accommodation. Warm welcome in a real
family home. Near the pub in a pretty
downland village just one mile from
The Ridgeway.

Harvesting

Wantage

⌖ **SU4088** ⊿ 4km (2.5 miles)
Market town with range of services

🚂 Didcot 13km (8 miles) 🅷

☆ Vale and Downland Museum
tel: 01235 771447

Lockinge Kiln Farm   *closed Xmas*

⌖ SU424834 1km (0.6miles) south of Ridgeway

Mrs Stella Cowan
Lockinge Kiln Farm, The Ridgeway, Chain Hill, WANTAGE, Oxon OX12 8PA
☎ 01235 763308 **Fax:** 01235 763308
Email: stellacowan@hotmail.com

🛏 1 🛏 2 £40.00 (£28.00) 🚭
V 🅰️🅾️ ⛾ 🅳🆁🆈 🕭 🚲

Ⓢ 3 £9.00 Ⓖ 6 £5.00

B & B In Wantage   *all year*

Mrs E Turner
B & B In Wantage, 50 Foliat Drive, WANTAGE, Oxon OX12 7AL
☎ 01235 760495 **Mob:** 07720 827325
Email: eleanor@eaturner.freeserve.co.uk

🛏 2 🛏 1 £36.00 (£20.00) 🚭 V 🅰
⛾ 🅳🆁🆈 🚗 🕭 🚲
🅷 Kitchen available to all rooms

The Bell Inn   *all year* 🄸🄽🄽

Mrs Sue Williams
The Bell Inn, 38 Market Place, WANTAGE, Oxon OX12 8AH
☎ 01235 763718 **Fax:** 01235 224392

🛏 2 🛏 2 🛏 7 £50.00 (£50.00)
🛏 5 £25.00 V 🅰🅾️🄱 ⛾
💳 Mastercard, Visa, American Express, Delta, Other

———— **Lockinge Kiln Farm** ————
The Ridgeway, Wantage, Oxfordshire ~ *Tel/Fax:* **01235 763308**
Comfortable farmhouse enjoying a quiet country location,
just ½ mile south of The Ridgeway. Ideal walking – riding – cycling.
Grid Reference: SU 424834

Ardington

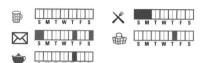

☷ Didcot 10km (6 miles) 📞

NB Post Office, shop & café also closed Sat & Sun afternoons in winter

☆ Ardington Pottery tel: 01235 833302

West Hendred

w-○-e
S **SU4488** 👢 4km (2.5 miles)

☷ Didcot 9km (6 miles) 📞

East Hendred

w-○-e
S **SU4688** 👢 4km (2.5 miles)

☷ Didcot 7km (4 miles) 📞

☆ Champs Chapel Museum tel: 01235 833315/833471

Cowdrays	*all year*

Mrs Margaret Bateman
Cowdrays, Cat Street, East Hendred,
WANTAGE, Oxon OX12 8JT
☎ 01235 833313 **Mob:** 07799 622003
Email: cowdrays@virgin.net

🛏 2 🛌 1 £52.00 (£30.00) 🚫 V 🎒
🔥 🚼 DRY 🚗 🦮 🚴

Monks Court	*all year*
U

Mrs Susie Turnbull
Monks Court, Newbury Road, East
Hendred, WANTAGE, Oxon OX12 8LG
☎ 01235 833797 **Mob:** 07710 274653
Fax: 01235 862554
Email: susie@monkscourt.demon.co.uk

🛏 1 🛌 1 £45.00 (£30.00) 🛏1 £25.00
🚫 V 🔥 🚼 ♿ DRY 🚗 🚴

Ⓖ 2-3 £3.00

West Ilsley

w-○-e
S **SU4782** 👢 2km (1.2 miles)

☷ Didcot 11km (7 miles) 📞

Chilton

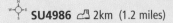 **SU4986** 2km (1.2 miles)

Didcot 6km (4 miles)

East Ilsley

 **SU4981** 2km (1.2 miles)

Didcot 11km (7 miles)

Upton

SU5186 4km (2.5 miles)

Didcot 5km (3 miles)

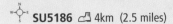

Compton

 **SU5280** 2km (1.2 miles)

Goring 9km (6 miles)

£ HSBC (Tue & Fri am only)

Compton Swan Hotel *all year*

Mr Garry Mitchell
Compton Swan Hotel, High Street,
Compton, NEWBURY, Berks RG20 6NJ
☎ 01635 578269 **Fax:** 01635 579630
Email:
garry@comptonswan.freeserve.co.uk
Website:
smoothhound.co.uk/hotels/comptons

1 4 1 £60.00 (£48.00)

V
Matercard, Visa, Delta

Blewbury

SU5385 4km (2.5 miles)

Didcot 6km (4 miles)

Aldworth

⌖ **SU5579** 🥾 2km (1.2 miles)

🚂 Goring 5km (3 miles) 📞

🍺 🔲🔲🔲🔲🔲🔲🔲
S M T W T F S
✕ 🔲🔲🔲🔲🔲🔲🔲
S M T W T F S

✉ ▮🔲🔲▮▮🔲🔲
S M T W T F S
🧺 🔲🔲🔲🔲🔲🔲🔲
S M T W T F S

Moulsford

⌖ **SU5983** 🥾 2km (1.2 miles)

🚂 Cholsey 3km (2 miles) 📞

🍺 🔲🔲🔲🔲🔲🔲🔲
S M T W T F S
✕ 🔲🔲🔲🔲🔲🔲🔲
S M T W T F S

🫖 🔲🔲🔲🔲🔲🔲🔲
S M T W T F S
🚫 🔲🔲🔲🔲🔲🔲🔲
S M T W T F S

White House   *closed Xmas, New Year*

Mrs Maria Watsham
White House, Moulsford-on-Thames,
WALLINGFORD, Oxon OX10 9JD
☎ 01491 651397 **Mob:** 07831 372243
Fax: 01491 652560
Email: mwatsham@cwcom.net

🛏 1 🛏 1 £50.00 (£35.00)
🛏 1£30.00 🚭 V 🏠🚫 👫 DRY 🚗 🚶
🚲 ◆◆◆◆

Streatley

⌖ **SU5980** on The Ridgeway

🚂 Goring 1km (0.5 miles) 📞

🍺 🔲🔲🔲🔲🔲🔲🔲
S M T W T F S
✕ 🔲🔲🔲🔲🔲🔲🔲
S M T W T F S

☆ Beale Park tel: 0118 9845172
Basildon Park tel: 0118 9843040

Pennyfield B & B   *closed Xmas, New Year*

Mrs Maureen Vanstone
Pennyfield B & B, The Coombe, Streatley,
READING, Berks RG8 9QT
☎ 01491 872048 **Fax:** 01491 872048
Email: mandrvanstone@hotmail.com
Website:
www.onetel.net.uk/~mandrvanstone

🛏 2 🛏 1 £55.00 (£55.00) 🚭 V 🏠
👫 over 10 years ♿ DRY 🚗 🚶 🚲
◆◆◆◆
🔪 ETC Silver Award, spa pool & en-suite
rooms

Harebells

YOUTH HOSTELS
Court Hill, Streatley, Bradenham and Ivinghoe

There are four Youth Hostels - at Court Hill, Streatley, Bradenham and Ivinghoe - along The Ridgeway National Trail, all offering affordable, friendly and comfortable accommodation in family rooms or dormitories. Prices start from £10.25 per night and meals are excellent value at £5.00 for evening and £3.40 for full breakfast. The YHA is a membership organisation; non-members are welcome to join on arrival at any Youth Hostel.

- Court Hill *Nr Wantage Letcombe Regis ? p58*
- Streatley
- Bradenham *? Sth of*
- Ivinghoe

P+ R's

Memorial window to John Betjeman by John Piper in Farnborough church

YHA Streatley *phone ahead*

The Manager
YHA Streatley, Hill House, Reading Road, Streatley, READING, Berks RG8 9JJ
☎ 01491 872278 **Fax:** 01491 873056
Email: streatley@yha.org.uk

🚭 V ⛺ 🌙 ♿ **DRY** 🚲
🛏 Dormitory accommodation £11.25/adult

Section 3

Streatley to Chinnor

This 33 km (21 miles) section of The Ridgeway in Oxfordshire is full of variety and charm. It passes through a couple of villages as it follows the River Thames before heading into the more wooded, yet still undulating, Chiltern Hills via an ancient Grim's Ditch and finishes on the wide track of the old Icknield Way.

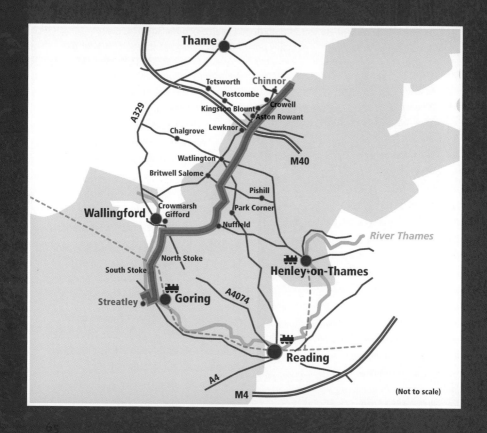

A Taster

Water, woodlands and small villages are features of this part of The Ridgeway, contrasting considerably with the open and more remote countryside of Sections One and Two.

England's most famous river, the River Thames, is your companion for the first few kilometres and as you follow it you'll pass through water meadows grazed by cattle and the two lovely villages of South and North Stoke. On the opposite bank, another National Trail runs, The Thames Path which The Ridgeway crossed at Goring bridge. Then as you strike east you'll walk on a narrow secluded path alongside a Grim's Ditch for a considerable distance, much of it surrounded by woodland bright with bluebells and wood anemones during spring.

From the village of Nuffield you turn north and soon reach the small hamlet of Swyncombe, an area which is probably one of the remotest and loveliest parts of the Chilterns. Here, the small flint church of St Botolph's has been beautifully restored.

Descending from Swyncombe to near the base of the scarp, The Ridgeway picks up the Upper Icknield Way and follows this broad track for the remaining 13 km (8 miles) to Chinnor. This latter part can be enjoyed by horseriders and cyclists as well as walkers and during wet times of the year gets muddy in places. The first 8 km (5 miles) of this Icknield Way section can also legally be used by drivers of vehicles.

Agriculture along this section is varied and includes a variety of crops and animal grazing. Many of the woodlands in the area, too, are managed for timber.

A few kilometres before Chinnor you'll cross the M40 by an underpass where the motorway slices through the Aston Rowant Nature Reserve in a deep cutting.

South Stoke church

History

The variety of landscape in this section is also reflected in the history of the area with the National Trail encountering amongst other things four important trading routes; the prehistoric Icknield Way, the River Thames used continuously for trading, the Great Western Railway constructed in the 19th century and, of course, today's motorway. The railway makes its impact unpleasantly felt as you initially walk north from Goring, but further along the Thames your path passes beneath Brunel's splendid bridge built in 1839 with its skewed arches and unusual brickwork - well worth a look.

Grim's Ditch is a fascinating ancient earthwork which accompanies you for several kilometres. It's amazing to think such a ditch was constructed using just antler picks as tools. Before you reach the Icknield Way you walk through several areas of woodland dominated by beech trees, and views of others stay with you to Chinnor.

Most of the beech trees you see today have been planted. From the 17th century the wood has been used, initially to supply a cheap source of fuel and charcoal for London and then in the last century by craftsmen. Tent-peg makers and chair leg turners, the bodgers, flourished throughout the Chilterns with the industry centred on High Wycombe. Few bodgers remain but the woodlands still have a commercial and leisure value.

As you pass Watlington it's worth looking to the south to the hillside rearing above you to spy the Watlington White Mark, another of the chalk figures cut into the hills through which The Ridgeway wanders.

Maps

Landranger maps	174	Newbury and Wantage
	175	Reading and Windsor
	165	Aylesbury and leighton Buzzard
Explorer maps	171	Chiltern Hills West

Public Transport Information

Rail Services   08457 484950 (24 hours a day)
www.railtrack.co.uk

Bus Services   0870 6082608
www.pti.org.uk

Taxis

Place	Name	Telphone Number
Goring	Murdock's Taxi Service	01491 872029
	M & S Taxis	01491 873253
Wallingford	Hills	01491 837022/837497
Benson	A Cabs	01491 839982
	Pontings Taxis	01491 826679
Ewelme	Bushers Taxis	01491 826161
Henley-on-Thames	Chiltern Taxis	01491 578899/577888
	County Cars	01491 579696
	Harris Taxis	01491 577036
Thame	English Chauffeur Drive	01844 260555/215483
	Bambrook Garage	01844 212885
	Thame Taxis	01844 216161/214433/215000
	T & B Private Hire	01844 261116
Chinnor	Chinnor Cabs	01844 353637
Bledlow Ridge	Ridge Rentals	01494 481568

Meadow cranesbill

Car Parking

The following are places close to or on The Ridgeway, other than villages or towns, with parking for vehicles - at some only for a few. Unfortunately theft from vehicles parked in the countryside does occasionally occur so please leave valuables at home.

Place	Map Grid Reference
Goring on Thames public car park	SU 599807
On Ridgeway on west side of minor road, 1.5 km (1 mile) southeast of Britwell Salome	SU 681922
On Ridgeway on east side of Hill Road, minor road to Christmas Common 1 km (0.5 miles) southeast of Watlington	SU 698940
On Ridgeway on east side of minor road to Bledlow Ridge 1 km (0.5 miles) south of Chinnor	SP 761003

Water Taps

- with troughs for animals

Place	Map Grid Reference
Grimsdyke Cottage, Grim's Ditch	SU 660872
Church, Nuffield (on the wall)	SU 667874

- White Mark Farm Camp Site, Watlington

(March-October)	SU 697939

Toilets

Place	Map Grid Reference
Goring-on-Thames (Car Park off Station Road)	SU 660872
White Mark Farm Camp Site, Watlington (March-October)	SU 697939
Watlington (High Street)	SU 689945

Police

Oxfordshire   01865 846000

Hospitals

Place	Telephone Number	Address
Wallingford	01491 835533	Wallingford Community Hospital, Reading Road, Wallingford.

Vets

Place	Name	Telephone Number
Wallingford	Dovecourt Group	01491 839043
Watlington	Crossroads	01491 612799
Thame/Chinnor	Sprinz and Nash	01844 212000
Kingston Blount	RE Baskerville	01844 352090

Farriers

Place	Name	Telephone Number
Chalgrove	Selwyn Mobile Farrier	07778 601831

Saddlers

Place	Name	Telephone Number
Stokenchurch	Equitana Equestrian	01494 484106

Mountain Bike Hire

Place	Name	Telephone Number
Wallingford	Rides on Air	01491 836289

Bike Repairs

Place	Name	Telphone Number
Pangbourne	Mountain High	0118 984 1851
Wallingford	Rides on Air	01491 836289
Thame	Thame Cycles	01844 261520

Tourist Information Centres

★ offers accommodation booking service

Place	Address/Opening Hours
★ Wallingford	Town Hall, Market Place, Wallingford OX10 0EG Tel: 01491 826972 Fax: 01491 832925 Opening hours: All year: Mon-Sat 09:30-17:00
★ Thame (★ Visitors to office only)	Market House, North Street, Thame OX9 3HH Tel/fax: 01844 212834 Opening hours: All year: Mon-Fri 09:30-17:00, Sat 10:00-16:00. Except: All Bank Holidays 10:00-15:00 August Sun 10:00-15:00

Grim's Ditch east of Wallingford

Goring Lock

Brunel's bridge between South and North Stoke

Goring

 SU6080 on The Ridgeway

🚂 Goring 📞 ♿WC

	S M T W T F S
🏦	⬜⬜⬜⬜⬜⬜⬜
✉️	⬛⬛⬜⬛⬛⬜⬜
☕	⬜⬜⬜⬜⬜⬜⬜
🗑	⬜⬜⬜⬜⬜⬜⬜

	S M T W T F S
✕	⬜⬜⬜⬜⬜⬜⬜
🧺	⬜⬜⬜⬜⬜⬜⬜
🗺	⬜⬜⬜⬜⬜⬜⬜

£ HSBC 🏧, Lloyds TSB

INN | **Miller of Mansfield** | *all year*

Mr M Williamson
Miller of Mansfield, High Street, Goring-on-Thames, READING, Berks RG8 9AW
☎ 01491 872829 **Fax:** 01491 874200
Website: www.millerofmansfield.co.uk

🛏 5 🛏 3 🛏 1 £75.00 (£57.50)
🛏 2 £57.50

V 🧗🚫🐕 ♿ 🚻 DRY 💳 Mastercard, Visa
◆◆◆

Northview House | *all year*

Mrs I Sheppard
Northview House, Farm Road, Goring-on-Thames, READING, Berks RG8 0AA
☎ 01491 872184 **Mob:** 07785 761851
Email:
hi@goring-on-thames.freeserve.co.uk

🛏 2 🛏 1 £40.00 (£20.00) 🚫🐕 🚻
DRY 🚶 🚲

South Stoke

 **SU6083** on The Ridgeway

🚂 Goring 3km (2 miles) 📞

	S M T W T F S
🍺	⬜⬜⬜⬜⬜⬜⬜

	S M T W T F S
✕	⬜⬜⬜⬜⬜⬜⬜

Perch & Pike, South Stoke

North Stoke

 SU6186 on The Ridgeway

🚆 Goring 6km (4 miles) 📞

Footpath Cottage *all year*

Mrs R G Tanner
Footpath Cottage, The Street, North Stoke,
WALLINGFORD, Oxon OX10 6BJ
☎ 01491 839763

🛏 1 £38.00 (£25.00) 🛏 1 £20.00 🚭
V 🥾🚫🗺 👫 **DRY** 🧒 🚲

Crowmarsh Gifford

 SU6189 1km (0.6 miles)

🚆 Didcot 10km (6 miles) 📞

 🍺 | S M T W T F S ✕ | S M T W T F S
✉ | S M T W T F S 🧺 | S M T W T F S

⚠ **Bridge Villa Caravan & Camp Site** *closed*

Mr E L Townsend
Bridge Villa, The Street, Crowmarsh
Gifford, WALLINGFORD, Oxon OX10 6MR
☎ 01491 836860 **Mob:** 07710 452429
Fax: 01491 839103
Email: ael.townsend@btinternet.com

⛺ 120 £5.00 🚐 120 £7.00 📱 🚰 🚿 ⓦ

💳 💳 💳 Mastercard, Visa, Delta

Wallingford

 SU6089 2km (1.2 miles)
Market town with range of services

🚆 Cholsey 9km (6 miles) ℹ

☆ Wallingford Museum tel: 01491
835065

Blenheim Farm House *closed Xmas New Year*
 SU636882 500m north of Ridgeway

Mrs Jeny Sarreti
Blenheim Farmhouse, Old Icknield Way,
WALLINGFORD, Oxon OX10 6PR
☎ 01491 832368
Email: peter.sarreti@which.net

🛏 1 £45.00 (£35.00) 🛏 1 £25.00 🚭
V 🥾 **DRY** 🚗 🧒 🚲

---

52 Blackstone Road *all year*

Mrs Enid J Barnard
52 Blackstone Road, WALLINGFORD, Oxon
OX10 8JL
☎ 01491 201917 **Email:**
enid.barnard@ebarnard.psnet.co.uk

🛏 1 £35.00 (£22.00) 🛏 1 £17.50 🚭
V **DRY** 🚗 🚲

Little Gables   *closed Xmas, New Year*

⚘ SU623889 1.2km (0.75miles) from Ridgeway

Mr & Mrs Reeves
Little Gables, 166 Crowmarsh Hill,
WALLINGFORD, Oxon OX10 8BG
☎ 01491 837834 **Mob:** 07860 148882
Fax: 01491 834426
Email: jill@stayingaway.com
Website: www.stayingaway.com

🛏 3 🛏 2 🛏 2 £50 - 55 (£35.00)
🛏 3 £35.00 🚭 V 🔥 🍴 ♿ **DRY** 🚶
🚲 ◆◆◆

Munts Mill   *all year*

Mrs Mary Broster
Munts Mill, Castle Lane, WALLINGFORD,
Oxon OX10 0BN
☎ 01491 836654

🛏 2 £22.50 🚭 V **DRY** 🚲
🚬 Advanced Bookings Only

Riverside Lodge   *all year*

Mrs Denise Tilbury
Riverside Lodge, 28 Preston Crowmarsh,
WALLINGFORD, Oxon OX10 6SL
☎ 01491 838093/838999
Mob: 07798 648807
Fax: 01491 838093
Email: davidjcleary@aol.com

🛏 1 £50.00 (£30.00) 🛏 1 £30.00 🚭
🔥 🍴 ♿ **DRY** 🚗 🚶 🚲

The George Hotel   *all year*

Mr Oliver Round-Turner
The George Hotel, High Street,
WALLINGFORD, Oxon OX10 0BS
☎ 01491 836665 **Fax:** 01491 825359
Email: info@george-hotel-wallingford.com **Website:** www.george-hotel-wallingford.com

🛏 1 £78.00 (£48.00) 🛏 9 £48.00
V 🔥 🕙 🍴 ♿ **DRY** 🚶 🚲
💳 Mastercard, Visa, American Express, Delta, Other ★ ★ ★
🚬 Smoking permitted in certain rooms only

The Studio   *all year*

Mrs Pamela Smith
The Studio, 85 Wantage Road,
WALLINGFORD, Oxon OX10 0LT
☎ 01491 837277
Email: bandb@prufit.co.uk
Website: pam@prufit.co.uk

🛏 1 🛏 1 £50.00 (£30.00)
🛏 2 £25.00 🚭 🕙 🍳 🍴 **DRY** 🚗 🚶
🚲

Nuffield

SU6787   on The Ridgeway

Henley 11km (7 miles)

☆ Nuffield Place tel: 01491 641224

Mays Farm	*all year*

SU654886 2km (1.2miles) from Ridgeway

Mrs P Passmore
Mays Farm, Nuffield, WALLINGFORD, Oxon
OX10 6QF
☎ 01491 641294/642056
Fax: 01491 641697

1 1 £42.00 (£30.00)
1 £25.00 V ♦♦♦

North of Swyncombe

Park Corner

SU6988 2km (1.2 miles)

Henley 10km (6 miles)

Parkcorner Farm House	*all year*

Mrs S M Rutter
Parkcorner Farm House, Park Corner,
Nettlebed, HENLEY-ON-THAMES, Oxon
RG9 6DX
☎ 01491 641450

2 £50.00 (£27.00) 1 £27.00
Free transport to pub

Pishill

SU7289 5km (3.1 miles)

Henley 9km (6 miles)

Bank Farm	*closed Xmas*

Mrs Elisabeth Lakey
Bank Farm, Pishill, HENLEY-ON-THAMES,
Oxon RG9 6HS
☎ 01491 638601 **Mob:** 07799 752933
Fax: 01491 638601
Email: bankfarm@btinternet.com

1 1 £48.00 (£20-24.00)
V ♦♦

Britwell Salome

⊕ **SU6787** 👢 1km (0.6 miles)

🚂 Henley 17km (11 miles) 📞

🍺 |⊞⊞⊞⊞⊞| S M T W T F S   ✉ |⊞⊞⊞⊞⊞| S M T W T F S

Huttons	*all year*

Mrs J Bowater
Huttons, Britwell Salome, WATLINGTON,
Oxon OX49 52H
☎ 01491 614389 **Mob:** 07736 270803
Fax: 01491 614993
Email: jbowater@etonwell.com

 2 £45.00 1 £48.00 (£25.00) 🚭
V 🖊️🅾️📷 🙌 **DRY** 🚗 🎿 🚲
💳 Mastercard, Visa, American Express,
Delta ◆◆◆

Watlington

⊕ **SU6894** 👢 1km (0.6 miles)

🚂 Henley 16km (10 miles) 📞 ♿WC

🍺 |⊞⊞⊞⊞⊞| S M T W T F S   🍴 |⊞⊞⊞⊞⊞| S M T W T F S
✉ |⊞⊞⊞⊞⊞| S M T W T F S   🛒 |⊞⊞⊞⊞⊞| S M T W T F S
🫖 |⊞⊞⊞⊞⊞| S M T W T F S   ✉ |⊞⊞⊞⊞⊞| S M T W T F S
🎁 |⊞⊞⊞⊞⊞| S M T W T F S

£ Barclays, Link cash machine in Co-Op

⊕ SU698939 50m from Ridgeway

Mrs R J Williams
White Mark Farm, 82 Hill Road,
WATLINGTON, Oxon OX49 5AF
☎ 01491 612295

⛺ many £6.00 🚐 5 £6.00 🚽 🚿 🚿 ♿
🦮 **DRY** 🚲

Woodgate Orchard Cottage	*all year*

Mrs Ronnie Roberts
Woodgate Orchard Cottage, Howe Road,
WATLINGTON, Oxon OX9 5EL
☎ 01491 612675 **Fax:** 01491 612675
Email: mailbox@wochr.freeserve.co.uk

2 2 £50.00 (£28.00) 🚭
V 🖊️🅾️🙌 🚫 **DRY** 🚗 🎿 🚲
🍴 Organic food

Watlington White Mark

Chalgrove

⊕ **SU6397** 👢 7km (4.4 miles)

🚆 Didcot 20km (12 miles) 📞

🍺 | S M T W T F S | ✕ | S M T W T F S |
✉ | S M T W T F S | 🧺 | S M T W T F S |

| **Cornerstones** | *closed Xmas, New Year* |

Mrs M Duxbury
Cornerstones, 1 Cromwell Close,
Chalgrove, OXFORD, Oxon OX44 7SE
☎ 01865 890298 **Mob:** 07808 658013
Fax: 01865 890298

🛏 2 £40.00 (£25.00) 🚭 V 🔥 ♿ 👫
🦽 **DRY** 🚗 🐾 🚲 ◆◆◆

The Icknield Way

Lewknor

⊕ **SU7197** 👢 1km (0.6 miles)

🚆 Princes Risborough 12km (7 miles) 📞

🍺 | S M T W T F S | ✕ | S M T W T F S |

☆ Cowleaze Wood Sculpture Trail

Bluebells

Tetsworth

⊕ **SP6801** 👢 6km (3.7 miles)

🚆 Princes Risborough 16km (10 miles) 📞

🍺 | S M T W T F S | ✕ | S M T W T F S |
✉ | S M T W T F S | 🍽 | S M T W T F S |
🏠 | S M T W T F S | | |

| **Little Acre B & B** | *all year* |

Ms Julia Tanner
Little Acre B & B, Tetsworth, THAME, Oxon
OX9 7AT
☎ 01844 281423 **Mob:** 07798 625252
Fax: 01844 281423
Email: julia@little-acre.co.uk
Website: www.little-acre.co.uk

🛏 2 £40.00 (£30.00) 🛏 1 £25.00
V 🔥 ♿ 👫 **DRY** 🚗 🚲

🚐 5 £6.00 📋 🔌 🚿 ♿

Postcombe

 SU7099 2.5km (1.6 miles)

Princes Risborough 13km (8 miles) **C**

	S M T W T F S		S M T W T F S

Beech Farm		*all year*

Mrs Jackie Graham
Beech Farm, Salt Lane, Postcombe, THAME,
Oxon OX9 7EE
☎ 01844 281240 **Mob:** 07973 506443
Fax: 01844 281240
Email: jackie.beech.farm.bb@talk21.com
Website:
www.ukworldnet/beechfarm.htm

🛏 1 ⚰ 2 £50.00 (£40.00) 🚫 **V** 🔥

Aston Rowant

 SU7298 1km (0.6 miles)

Princes Risborough 10km (6 miles) **C**

	S M T W T F S		S M T W T F S

Peel Guest House		*all year*

Mrs Elaine Hunt
Peel Guest House, London Road, ASTON
ROWANT, Oxon OX49 5SA
☎ 01844 351310

2 £45.00 (£30.00) 1 £25.00 **V** 🔥

Kingston Blount

SU7399 0.8km (0.5 miles)

Princes Risborough 10km (6 miles) **C**

	S M T W T F S		S M T W T F S

Crowell

SU7409 0.8km (0.5 miles)

Princes Risborough 9km (5.6 miles) **C**

	S M T W T F S		S M T W T F S

Near Kingston Blount

Chinnor

SP7500 👢 1km (0.6 miles)

🚂 Princes Risborough 7km (4 miles)

📞 ♿

☆ Chinnor and Princes Risborough Steam Railway tel: 01844 353535

Caring for the Chilterns

You can help the Chilterns by

The Chilterns
Area of Outstanding Natural Beauty

- Enjoying, understanding and caring for the chilterns
- Leaving your car at home
- Showing respect to other users of the countryside
- Supporting the local economy - buy local products and services
- Not disrupting the activities of those who make their living from the countryside
- Taking pride in the Chilterns - follow the Country Code

Section 4

Chinnor to Ivinghoe Beacon

This 37 km (23 miles) eastern stretch of The Ridgeway wanders its way through wonderful wooded parts of the Chiltern Hills before emerging, just a few kilometres from its finish, into more open downland countryside reminiscent of the landscape surrounding its earlier stages. Keeping mainly to quiet footpaths, the Trail skirts around or dips into a few Chiltern settlements where welcome refreshments are easily available.

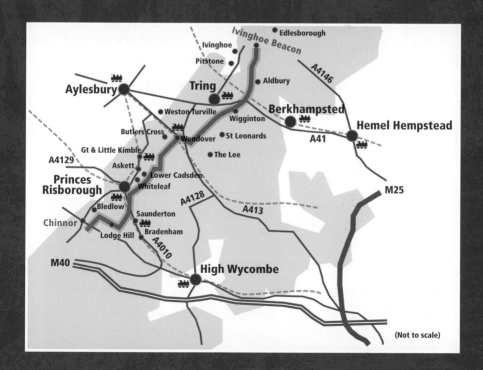

Edlesborough
Ivinghoe Beacon
Ivinghoe
Pitstone
A4146
Tring
Aldbury
Aylesbury
Weston Turville
Berkhampsted
Hemel Hempstead
Wigginton
Butlers Cross
Wendover
St Leonards
A41
Gt & Little Kimble
The Lee
A4129
Askett
Princes Risborough
Lower Cadsden
Whiteleaf
M25
Bledlow
A4128
A413
Chinnor
Saunderton
Lodge Hill
Bradenham
A4010
M40
High Wycombe

(Not to scale)

A Taster

Dominated by fine beech woodlands for which the Chiltern Hills are justly famous, this countryside however offers more than just trees. Probably the most undulating with several usually reasonably gentle climbs in and out of valleys, this section of The Ridgeway gives some marvellous experiences.

One minute you may be walking up a sheltered slope amongst the tall, straight, grey trunks of beeches and the next you'll have emerged into some fine unimproved chalk grassland boasting a great variety of wild flowers and insects with tremendous views across the Vale of Aylesbury. Or, turning a corner you'll reach the edge of a wood and have a view, framed by branches, of a secluded valley with just a small brick and timber farm complex nestling below you.

Agriculture is varied with crops grown in places, and sheep, cattle and horses grazed elsewhere. Many places are in fact nature reserves where the sheep and cattle are essential elements of the management to ensure the traditional chalk grasslands remain free of scrub and rich in wild species. The woodlands, too, are not just places for leisure as many are managed commercially for their timber.

You pass close to Princes Risborough and through the centre of Wendover, both typical and attractive small Chilterns towns, as well as going near some lovely villages. On Coombe Hill, marked by its monument, you will find yourself at the highest point of the Chiltern Hills with views on a clear day, extending as far as the Berkshire Downs and the Cotswolds. Just beyond Tring you reach the busy A41 trunk road but you cross it high above on a bridge specially built to carry The Ridgeway and it's soon forgotten.

Looking towards Ivinghoe Beacon from Pitstone Hill

History

There's plenty of historical interest to explore close to the route you follow in this section.

For those interested in prehistoric sites, there are long and round barrows, Iron Age forts, and sections of Grim's Ditch to seek out. The oldest barrow, a New Stone Age long barrow at least 4000 years old, is located on Whitelaf Hill just a stone's throw from the Cross cut in the chalk of the north facing slope. For those skilled at finding them, Bronze Age round barrows dating roughly from 2000 to 750 BC, exist in many places with the most obvious situated just to the north of the path at the bottom of the slope up to Ivinghoe Beacon.

And once you reach your journey's end at the top of Beacon Hill itself, there's an Iron Age fort to greet you. Earlier you will have skirted the edge of a similar fort on Pulpit Hill north of the small village of Lower Cadsden. On Pitstone Hill as you emerge from the woodland of Aldbury Nowers, you walk for a while on the edge of a section of Grim's Ditch. This one, unlike that in section 3, is in the open surrounded by chalk grassland.

There is also ample evidence of Man's more recent activities. There are chalk figures cut into the side of the hills at Bledlow and Whitelaf, a memorial to the men of Buckinghamshire who died during the Boer War in South Africa at the turn of this century atop the highest point in the Chilterns, Coombe Hill, and two important country houses, Chequers, the Prime Minister's country residence, and Tring Park close to the Trail.

Maps

Landranger maps	165	Aylesbury and Leighton Buzzard
Explorer maps	181	Chiltern Hills North

Public Transport Information

Rail Services   08457 484950 (24 hours a day)
           www.railtrack.co.uk

Bus Services   0870 6082608
           www.pti.org.uk

Taxis

Place	Name	Telphone Number
Chinnor	Chinnor Cabs	01844 353637
Bledlow Ridge	Ridge Rentals	01494 481568
Princes Risborough	B & V Taxis	01844 342079
	Elite	01844 274800
	Red Line Car Hire	01844 343736
	Village Cars	01844 342551
High Wycombe	0001 Wycombe Taxis	01494 463360
	A Cars	01494 523344
	A1 Taxi Service	01494 441000
	Tiger Taxis	01494 461111
Wendover	Chilton Taxis	01296 624838
Wigginton	Barrington Taxis	01442 823263
Aylesbury	001 Emergency Cabs	01296 339999
	A1 Taxis	01296 425555/489777
	A to B Taxis	01296 399299
	Eagles Cars	01296 422121
Tring	A1 John Taxis	01442 828828
	Bev's Cars	01442 824105
	Mike's Private Hire	01442 826161

Car Parking

The following are places close to or on The Ridgeway, other than villages or towns, with parking for vehicles - at some only for a few. Unfortunately theft from vehicles parked in the countryside does occasionally occur so please leave valuables at home.

Place	Map Grid Reference
On Ridgeway on east side of minor road to Bledlow Ridge 1 km (0.5 miles) south of Chinnor	SP 761003
Princes Risborough public car park	SP 810034
Whitelaf car park, 1 km (0.5 miles) east of Princes Risborough. Turn right off A4010 at Monks Risborough and car park is on left at top of escarpment	SP 824036
National Trust car park for Coombe Hill, 2 km (1 mile) southwest of Wendover. From Wendover travel west on minor road to Princes Risborough. Take first left then first left again. At top of hill car park is on left.	SP 852062
Wendover public car park	SP 868077
Pitstone Hill car park east of Tring. From sharp bend on B488, 1 km (0.5 miles) southeast of Ivinghoe, take minor road signposted Aldbury. Car park is on right after 1 km (0.5 miles)	SP 955149
National Trust car park for Ivinghoe Beacon, on the left of minor road to Ringshall, 1 km (0.5 miles) south off the B489	SP 962162

Toilets

Place	Map Grid Reference
Princes Risborough (Horn Mill Car Park)	SP 809033
Wendover (Library Car Park)	SP 868078

Police

Oxfordshire and Buckinghamshire	01865 846000
Hertfordshire	01707 354200

Hospitals

Place	Telphone Number	Address
Aylesbury	01296 315000	Stoke Mandeville Hospital, Mandeville Road, Aylesbury.

Vets

Place	Name	Telphone Number
Princes Risborough	Sprinz and Nash	01844 345655
Aylesbury (equine)	Baskerville, Morgan and partners	01296 432633
Wendover	Wendover Heights	01296 623439
Tring	Springwell	01442 822151

Farriers

Place	Name	Telphone Number
Aylesbury	A E Speller	01296 393896
Berkhamsted	Mark Rudge	01442 879472

Saddlers

Place	Name	Telphone Number
Chartridge (near The Lee)	Chris Gohl	01494 837138
Westcott	Balance	01296 658333
Aylesbury	Dennis's	01296 658660

Mountain Bike Hire

Place	Name	Telphone Number
Princes Risborough	Boltons Bikes	01844 345949

Bike Repairs

Place	Name	Telphone Number
Princes Risborough	Boltons Bikes	01844 345949
Aylesbury	Buckingham Bikes	01296 822201
High Wycombe	Cycle Care	01494 447908
Berkhamsted	Dees Cycles	01442 877447
Dunstable	Dysons Cycles	01582 665533

Tourist Information Centres

★ offers accommodation booking service

Place	Address/Opening Hours
★ Thame (★ Visitors to office only)	Market House, North Street, Thame OX9 3HH Tel/fax: 01844 212834 Opening hours: All year: Mon-Fri 09:30-17:00, Sat 10:00-16:00. Except: All Bank Holidays 10:00-15:00 August Sun 10:00-15:00
Princes Risborough	Tower Court, Horns Lane, Princes Risborough HP27 OAJ Tel: 01844 274795 Fax: 01844 275795 Opening hours: All year: Mon-Fri 09:00-17:00
★ Wendover (★ until 15:30)	Clock Tower, High Street, Wendover HP22 6AA Tel: 01296 696759 Fax: 01296 622460 Opening hours: All year: Mon-Sat 10:00-16:00
Tring	99 Akeman Street, Tring HP23 6AA Tel/Fax: 01442 823347 email: tring@mildram.co.uk Opening hours: All year: Mon-Fri 09:30-15:00, Sat 10:00-13:00
Berkhamsted	c/o Berkhamsted Library, Kings Road, Berkhamsted HP4 3BD Tel: 01438 737333 (ask for Berkhamsted Library) Opening hours: All year: Mon 09:30-17:30, Tue 10:30-20:00, Wed closed, Thu 09:30-20:00, Fri 09:30-17:30, Sat 09:30-16:00
Dunstable	c/o Dunstable Library, Vernon Place, Dunstable LU5 4HA Tel: 01582 471012 Fax: 01582 471290 Opening hours: All year: Mon-Fri 10:00-17:00, Sat 09:30-16:00

4 Chinnor to Ivinghoe Beacon

Bledlow

⌖ **SP7702** 🥾 1km (0.6 miles)

🚂 Princes Risborough 3km (2 miles) 📞

🍺 [|||||||||||] × [|||||||||||]
  S M T W T F S   S M T W T F S

Lodge Hill

⌖ **SP7900**   on The Ridgeway

🚂 Princes Risborough 3km (2 miles)

Old Callow Down Farm *all year*

⌖ SU698939 50m from Ridgeway

Mr & Mrs C J Gee
Old Callow Down Farm, Wigans Lane,
Bledlow Ridge, HIGH WYCOMBE, Bucks
HP14 4BH
☎ 01844 344416 **Fax:** 01844 344703
Email: oldcallow@aol.com
Website: www.chilternscottage.co.uk

🛏 1 🛏 1 £44.00 (£30.00) 🛏1 £25.00
🚫 V 🔥 🚫 🔳 ⛎ DRY 🔁 ⚲

View from Lodge Hill

Saunderton

SP7901 🥾 1km (0.6 miles)

🚂 Princes Risborough 2km (1 miles)

🍺 |||||||||||| S M T W T F S ✕ |||||||||||| S M T W T F S

Hunters Gate B & B   *all year*

Mrs Anne Dykes
Hunters Gate, Dernfield, Saunderton, HIGH
WYCOMBE, Bucks HP14 4JR
☎ 01494 481718
Email: dadykes@attglobal.net

🛏 1   🛏 1 £40.00 (£30.00) 🚭 V 🧴
📶 ⚤ DRY 🚗 🎒 🚲◆◆◆

Ⓢ 2 £5.00 Ⓖ 4 £5.00

Bradenham

SU8297 🥾 5km (3.1 miles)

🚂 Saunderton 2km (1 miles) 📱

🍺 |||||||||||| S M T W T F S ✕ ||||||||||| S M T W T F S

YHA Bradenham   *phone ahead*

The Manager
YHA Bradenham, The Village Hall,
Bradenham, HIGH WYCOMBE, Bucks HP14
4HF
☎ 01494 562929 **Fax:** 01494 564743
Email: bradenham@yha.org.uk

🚭 🧴 ⚤ ♿ DRY 🚲
🛏 Dormitory accommodation, price on
application

Princes Risborough

SP8003   on The Ridgeway
Market town with range of services

🚂 Princes Risborough 📶

The Black Prince   *all year* INN

Mr Simon Keen
The Black Prince, 86 Wycombe Road,
PRINCES RISBOROUGH, Bucks HP27 0EN
☎ 01844 345569 **Fax:** 01844 345076
Email: black.prince@tesco.net

🛏 2   🛏 4 £55.00 (£35.00) 🛏 3 £35.00
V 🧴 🚭 📶 ⚤ DRY 🎒 🚲 💳
Mastercard, Visa, Delta, Other
🛏 All rooms en-suite

Whiteleaf

⊕ SP8204 🥾 1km (0.6 miles)

🚃 Monks Risborough 1.5km (1 miles)

🍺 ▮▯▯▯▯▯▯▯ ╳ ▮▮▯▯▯▯▯▯
   S M T W T F S   S M T W T F S

Lower Cadsden

⊕ SP8204 on The Ridgeway

🚃 Monks Risborough 2km (1 miles)

🍺 ▯▯▯▯▯▯▯▯ ╳ ▯▯▯▯▯▯▯▯
   S M T W T F S   S M T W T F S

Askett

⊕ SP8105 🥾 2km (1.2 miles)

🚃 Monks Risborough 1km (0.5 miles)

🍺 ▯▯▯▯▯▯▯▯ ╳ ▮▮▯▯▯▯▯▯
   S M T W T F S   S M T W T F S

Solis Ortu   *all year*

Mrs Pamela Crockett
Solis Ortu, Aylesbury Road, Askett,
PRINCES RISBOROUGH, Bucks HP27 9LY
☎ 01844 344175 **Fax:** 01844 343509

🛏 2 🛏 1 £45.00 (£25.00) 🚭 ♨
👫 🚗 🚲 ♦♦♦

Great Kimble

⊕ SU8206 🥾 1km (0.6 miles)

🚃 Little Kimble 1km (0.5 miles) 📞

🍺 ▯▯▯▯▯▯▯▯ ╳ ▯▯▯▯▯▯▯▯
   S M T W T F S   S M T W T F S
✂ ▯▯▯▯▯▯▯▯ 🗑 ▮▮▮▮▮▮▮▮
   S M T W T F S   S M T W T F S

Butlers Cross

⊕ SP8407 🥾 1km (0.6 miles)

🚃 Little Kimble 2km (1 miles) 📞

🍺 ▮▯▯▯▯▯▯▯ ╳ ▮▮▯▯▯▯▯▯
   S M T W T F S   S M T W T F S

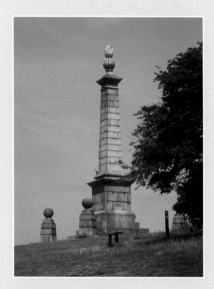

Monument on Coombe Hill

Wendover

⌖ **SP8607** on The Ridgeway

🚃 Wendover 📞 ♿WC 🛈

£ Lloyds TSB ▣, Barclays ▣
☆ Wendover Woods tel: 01296 625825

Belton House   *closed Xmas, New Year*

Mrs E C Condie
Belton House, 26 Chiltern Road,
WENDOVER, Bucks HP22 6DB
☎ 01296 622351

🛏 1 £30.00 (£20.00) 🛏 1 £15.00 🚭
🔲 🕴 DRY ◆

Dunsmore Edge   *closed Xmas, New Year*

⌖ SP875057 1.6km (1mile) from
Ridgeway

Mr & Mrs R A Drackford
Dunsmore Edge, Dunsmore Lane, London
Road, WENDOVER, Bucks HP22 6PN
☎ 01296 623080
Email: uron@lineone.net

🛌 3 🛏 1 £45.00 (£25.00) 🚭
V 🚵 DRY 🚗 🚲 ◆◆◆

Mrs MacDonald's   *closed Xmas, New Year*

Mr G MacDonald
Mrs MacDonald's, 46 Lionel Avenue,
Wendover, AYLESBURY, Bucks HP22 6LP
☎ 01296 623426

🛏 1 £48.00 (£25.00) 🛏 2 £24.00 🚭
V 🚵 🔲 🕴 DRY 🚶 🚲 ◆◆◆

Weston Turville

⌖ **SP8611** ⌂ 3km (1.9 miles)

🚃 Wendover 4km (2 miles) 📞

The Hamlet B & B   *all year*

Mrs Maria Burgess
The Hamlet B & B, 3 Home Close, Weston
Turville, AYLESBURY, Bucks HP22 5SP
☎ 01296 612660 **Mob:** 07889 247903
Fax: 01296 612660
Email: gburg27705@aol.com

🛏 1 🛏 1 £50.00 (£35.00) 🛏 1 £25.00
🚭 🕴 DRY 🚲 💳 Mastercard, Visa,
Delta ◆◆◆

The Lee

$\oplus$ **SP9004** 🥾 3km (1.9 miles)

🚂 Wendover 6km (4 miles) 📞

🍺 |SMTWTFS| ✕ |SMTWTFS|
✉ |SMTWTFS|

Patchwicks *all year*

Mrs J Syer
Patchwicks, The Lee, GREAT MISSENDEN,
Bucks HP16 9LZ
☎ 01494 837596

🛏 1 🛌 1 £48.00 (£26.00) 🚭
V 🏕🚫👪 DRY 🚗 🔦🚲

St Leonards

$\oplus$ **SP9107** 🥾 1.5km (0.9 miles)

🚂 Wendover 5km (3 miles) 📞

🍺 |SMTWTFS| ✕ |SMTWTFS|

Field Cottage *closed Xmas, New Year*
$\oplus$ SP900063 600m from Ridgeway

Mrs Susan Jepson
Field Cottage, St Leonards, TRING, Herts
HP23 6NS
☎ 01494 837602

🛏 1 🛌 1 £55.00 (£35.00)
🛏 1 £35.00 🚭 V 👪 over 12 years DRY
🚲 ♦♦♦♦
🏅 ETC Silver Award

Bacombe Hill west of Wendover

Wigginton

⊕ **SP9310**   on The Ridgeway

🚆 Tring 2km (1 miles) 📞

🍺 |S M T W T F S| 🍴 |S M T W T F S|

| **Rangers Cottage** | *all year* |

Mrs Sally Dawson
Rangers Cottage, Tring Park, Wigginton,
TRING, Herts HP23 6EB
☎ 01442 890155 **Fax:** 01442 827814
Email: rangerscottage@aol.com

🛏 2 🛏 1 £58.00 (£35.00) 🚭 V 🏔
👫 DRY 🚲 VISA Mastercard, Visa
◆◆◆◆
All rooms en-suite

Tring

⊕ **SP9211** 🥾 2km (1.2 miles)
Small town with range of services

🚆 Tring 🛈

☆ Tring Zoological Museum tel: 01442
824181

Aldbury

⊕ **SP9612** 🥾 1km (0.6 miles)

🚆 Tring 1.5km (1 miles) 📞

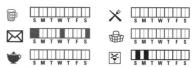

NB Shop closed Sun afternoon in winter

☆ Ashridge Estate tel: 01442 842488

| **16 Stoneycroft** | *closed Xmas, New Year* |

Mrs Sandra Crannage
16 Stoneycroft, Aldbury, TRING, Herts HP23
5RL
☎ 01442 851294 **Mob:** 07801 846351
Fax: 01442 851294

🛏 1 £30.00 (£20.00) 🛏 1 £20.00 🚭

Pitstone

⊕ **SP9315** 🥾 2.5km (1.6 miles)

🚆 Tring 4km (2 miles) 📞

🍺 |S M T W T F S| 🧺 |S M T W T F S|
🍴 |S M T W T F S| 🛒 |S M T W T F S|

☆ Pitstone Green Museum. Pitstone
Windmill tel: 01494 528051

Ivinghoe

☼ **SP9416** ⌂ 1.5km (0.9 miles)

🚂 Tring 5km (3 miles) 📞

🍺 |||||||||| S M T W T F S   ✕ |||||||||| S M T W T F S

✉ |||||||||| S M T W T F S   🧺 |||||||||| S M T W T F S

☆ Ford End Watermill tel: 01582 600391

YHA Ivinghoe　　　　*phone ahead*

The Manager
YHA Ivinghoe, The Old Brewery House,
High Street, IVINGHOE, Beds LU7 9EP
☎ 01296 668251 **Fax:** 01296 662903
Email: ivinghoe@yha.org.uk

🚫 V 🏍 🕭 ♥♥ DRY 🚲
▒ Mastercard, Visa, Delta
🛏 Dormitory accommodation £10.25/adult

Edlesborough

☼ **SP9719** ⌂ 3km (1.9 miles)

🚂 Tring 9km (6 miles) 📞

🍺 |||||||||| S M T W T F S   ✕ |||||||||| S M T W T F S

✉ |||||||||| S M T W T F S   🧺 |||||||||| S M T W T F S

Ridgeway End　　*closed Xmas, New Year*

Mrs Judith Lloyd
Ridgeway End, 5 Ivinghoe Way,
Edlesborough, DUNSTABLE, Beds LU6 2EL
☎ 01525 220405 **Mob:** 07721 027339
Fax: 01525 220405

🛏2 🛏1 🛏1£48.00 (£28.00) 🚫 V
🏍 🕭 ♥♥ DRY 🚗 🐾 🚲

North of Tring Station

Aldbury	93	Marlborough	37
Aldworth	63	Moulsford	63
Ardington	61	North Stoke	74
Ashbury	45	Nuffield	76
Askett	90	Ogbourne St George	42
Aston Rowant	79	Park Corner	76
Avebury	38	Pishill	76
Barbury Castle	38	Pitstone	93
Bishopstone	44	Postcombe	79
Bledlow	88	Princes Risborough	89
Blewbury	62	Saunderton	89
Bradenham	89	South Stoke	73
Britwell Salome	77	Sparsholt	57-58
Broad Hinton	38	St Leonards	92
Butlers Cross	90	Streatley	63-64
Chalgrove	78	Swindon	41
Childrey	58	Tetsworth	78
Chilton	62	The Lee	92
Chinnor	80	Tring	93
Chiseldon	41	Uffington	48
Compton	62	Upton	62
Crowell	79	Wallingford	74
Crowmarsh Gifford	74	Wanborough	43
East Hendred	61	Wantage	43
East Ilsley	62	Watlington	77
Edlesborough	94	Wendover	91
Faringdon	48	West Hendred	61
Goring	73	West Ilsley	61
Great Kimble	90	Weston Turville	91
Ivinghoe	94	West Overton	37
Kingston Blount	79	Whiteleaf	90
Kingston Lisle	57	Wigginton	93
Letcombe Regis	58-59	Winterbourne Bassett	38
Lewknor	78	Winterbourne Monkton	38
Liddington	42	Woolstone	46
Lodge Hill	88	Wroughton	41
Lower Cadsden	90		

Distances between places along the The Ridgeway in miles

	Overton Hill	Ogbourne St George	Fox hill	Uffington Castle	A338 (Wantage)	Bury Down	Streatley	Mongewell Park	Nuffield	Watlington	Chinnor	Princes Risborough	Wendover	Wigginton
Ogbourne St George	9.1													
Fox hill	16.5	7.4												
Uffington Castle	21.9	12.8	5.4											
A338 (Wantage)	28.2	19.1	11.7	6.3										
Bury Down	33.9	24.8	17.4	12.0	5.7									
Streatley	42.0	32.9	25.5	20.1	13.8	8.1								
Mongewell Park	47.7	38.6	31.2	25.8	19.5	13.8	5.7							
Nuffield	51.7	42.6	35.2	29.8	23.5	17.8	9.7	4.0						
Watlington	57.1	48.0	40.6	35.2	28.9	23.2	15.1	9.4	5.4					
Chinnor	62.7	53.6	46.2	40.8	34.5	28.8	20.7	15.0	11.0	5.6				
Princes Risborough	68.0	58.9	51.5	46.1	39.8	34.1	26.0	20.3	16.3	10.9	5.3			
Wendover	73.9	64.8	57.4	52.0	45.7	40.0	31.9	26.2	22.2	16.8	11.2	5.9		
Wigginton	80.0	70.9	63.5	58.1	51.8	46.1	38.0	32.3	28.3	22.9	17.3	12.0	6.1	
Ivinghoe Beacon	85.5	76.4	69.0	63.6	57.3	51.6	43.5	37.8	33.8	28.4	22.8	17.5	11.6	5.5